RAGING
HORMONES

RAGING HORMONES

WHAT TO DO WHEN YOU SUSPECT YOUR TEEN MAY BE SEXUALLY ACTIVE.

Jack & Judith Balswick

ZondervanPublishingHouse

Grand Rapids, Michigan

A Division of HarperCollinsPublishers

Raging Hormones
Copyright © 1994 by Judith and Jack Balswick

Requests for information should be addressed to:
Zondervan Publishing House
Grand Rapids, Michigan 49530

Library of Congress Cataloging-in-Publication Data Balswick, Judith K.
   Raging Hormones : what to do when you suspect your teen may be
sexually active / Judith and Jack Balswick
      p.   cm.
   ISBN 0-310-59591-6
   1. Sex instruction for youth–Religious aspects–Christianity. 2. Sexual
ethics for youth. 3. Parent and teenager. I. Balswick, Jack O. II. Title.
MHQ35.B325 1994   94-10884
M306.7'0835–dc20   CIP

Scripture taken from the HOLY BIBLE: NEW INTERNATIONAL VER-
SION® (North American Edition). Copyright © 1973, 1978, 1984, by the
International Bible Society. Used by permission of Zondervan Publishing
House.

The "NIV" and "New International Version" trademarks are registered in the
United States Patent and Trademark Office by the International Bible Society.
Use of either trademark requires the permission of International Bible Society.

Edited by Jeron Frame
Cover design by John M. Lucas
Cover photo by Jon Feingersh, The Stock Market

Printed in the United States of America

94 95 96 97 98 / DH / 9 8 7 6 5 4 3 2 1

Contents

Preface

It is estimated that 43% of churched kids have sex by age 18! Although your teenager may not be a part of this statistic, it is easy to deny the signs that one's child is sexually involved. After all, we, as parents, have a vested interest in not "seeing" reality when it differs from what we want it to be. In dealing with what *is* rather than what should be, this book is an attempt to help parents address the topic of sexually active teenagers in a realistic and compassionate way.

There are few discoveries that are more threatening to parents' relationships with their teenage children than premarital sexual behavior. Discovering that your teenager is sexually involved brings forth feelings of shock, betrayal, shame, and rage that often prevent you from interacting with them in effective ways about the issues involved. This book will help you deal with the feelings that arise when you face the truth about your teenager's sexual involvement, so you can honestly dialogue with them toward constructive solutions at a critical time in their life.

Your teen needs to realize the risks that are involved in being sexually active. While you may totally disagree with your child's sexual involvement, you nonetheless need to instruct your child so he or she won't make a life-threatening mistake. This book will help you communicate the risks of sexual involvement—sexually transmitted diseases, unplanned pregnancy, emotional scarring—and ways of reducing these life-threatening risks.

You need to prepare yourself for the fact that, as part of the "just do it" generation, your teen may make unwise choices in the adolescent sexual wilderness. But we also believe that you can guide them out of that wilderness into a deeper understanding of why premarital abstinence is a mature choice. Your children need to know that while they can never erase the past, they can "reclaim their virginity" by committing themselves to celibacy.

Acknowledgments

We thank our parents, who are now in their 80s, for modeling healthy loving relationships for neary 60 years, and to our children, Jacque and Joel, who have taught us so much about parenting. We also thank Lyn Cryderman for coming up with the idea of writing this book and for giving us many valuable suggestions. We greatly appreciate the editorial work done by Rachel Boers for putting her creative touches on the finished product.

1

Parental Denial:
Not My Child!

Dave and his steady girlfriend, Stephanie, spent Christmas break at his parents' home. One morning, while doing laundry, Mrs. Johnson found a condom in the pocket of her son's jeans. Although separate sleeping arrangements had been carefully planned and guidelines spelled out, Dave and Stephanie obviously didn't let this interfere with their sexual relationship. When confronted by his parents, Dave explained, "It's common practice at college." Mr. Johnson went into a rage. He demanded that Stephanie leave and threatened to withdraw financial support for Dave's schooling.

Sixteen-year-old Tammy, daughter of Karen Dubose, was disrupted by her mother's unexpected appearance. Karen had left work early that day with flu symptoms only to find Tammy and her boyfriend in bed together. Caught in the act, they fumbled around with half-baked explanations. It was a horrible scene! Karen slammed the door, retreated into her bedroom and lamented the woes of being a single parent. It was hard enough trying to deal with her own sexuality, let alone her teenage daughter's. She was at a loss as to what to do.

These are the familiar stories of parents who come to us for counseling about their teenager's sexual activities. If you've had a similar experience with your teenager, let us assure you that no parent is ever prepared to learn that their adolescent is engaging in sexual intercourse. It seems like only yesterday that we were wiping noses and driving our kids to grammar school. Mending a scraped elbow with a kiss and a band-aid was a quick and easy remedy, but now the stakes are higher. It's not so simple to fix the hurts of unwise sexual decisions. Anxieties you may feel about your teenager's sexual involvement are not unfounded, for their raging hormones are a powerful force that can lead them to make irreversible mistakes!

From Innocence to Awareness

It's understandable to want to ignore the tell-tale signs when our adolescent first begins experimenting with sexual thoughts, feelings, and actions. Those hormones announce what we've tried so hard to deny—that our innocent child is becoming a sexually potent adolescent. The time and energy we've invested in protecting and caring for our young child recedes into the background as we watch our adolescent make decisions about sexual matters without looking to us for advice.

It takes only a few short years for the boy/girl antagonisms and cries of "ewww, cooties!" to change to furtive glances and shy handholding. Do you remember the day you realized your child wasn't a kid anymore? If your adolescent has gone way beyond the handholding stage, you know how quickly and powerfully those hormones can kick in.

Teens tend to live for the moment, doing what feels good without thinking through the ramifications of their behavior. It's scary to listen to the naive, cavalier attitudes when you consider the enormous risks teenagers take. Jenna, a 16-year-old high school student and pregnant for the second time, describes her situation in a fatalistic way. "I guess it was meant to be," she says. "God has everything planned, so this is what He planned for my life." Did Jenna really believe she was exempt from the dangers of sexually transmitted diseases or complications of bringing a child into the world? Had it not occurred to her that she was responsible for her pregnancy? On the same program, a young boy with the HIV virus reminded the TV audience, "We're not bulletproof just because we have the basic facts about sex! We have feelings and needs for loving that must be addressed."

How can you address the feelings and needs your teenagers have about sex and love after they've been sexually active? This is the question our book addresses. In order for you to know what to say and how to say it, you'll need be familiar with what's really happening for teenagers when it comes to sexual activity.

Just the Facts Ma'am

Would it surprise you to hear that two-thirds of American teenagers today are having sex with more than one partner? It's estimated that about seventy percent of 18-year-olds are sexually active. It's easy for us to shake our heads about what's happening in the world, but when our own teenager is involved, the facts are even harder to swallow. Christian youth are *not* exempt. While research indicates that young people who have strong religious beliefs are more conservative in their attitudes and behaviors regarding sexual expression, they also grapple with the same social and peer pressures. Let's take a moment to look at some recent research regarding teenage sexual behavior in the United States.

According to a report released in 1992 by the Center for Disease Control, over half of high school students in the United States have had sex. This study, based on responses of 11,631 students, found that the percentage of those having sex climbed from 40% for ninth graders, to 48% for 10th graders, to 57% for 11th graders, and finally to 72% of 12th graders. More boys (61%) reported having had sex than girls (48%), while 53% of white students, 52% of hispanic students, and 72% of black students reported having had sex.

A study by Miller and Moore in 1990 reported that by age nineteen, 80% of unmarried females and 86% of unmarried males have engaged in sexual intercourse. Just how many of those young persons are from Christian homes is a matter of speculation. But after talking to students from Christian colleges scattered throughout the United States, it appears that many of them are sexually active. A 1992 study concluded that church attendance on the part of teens "played a significant role in moderating the effects of early sexual intercourse." In a survey conducted by Josh McDowell Ministries, it was found that 43% of teens growing up in church-going families have sex by age 18. Christian teenagers may engage in premarital sex less than non-Christian teens, but at least 4 out of 10 Christian adolescents will have premarital sex before they leave their teenage years.

This should confirm your suspicions that you're not alone in this matter! Many Christian parents are struggling with what to do and say to their teenagers about the sexual decisions they make. If sex is such a stumbling block for our teens, why did God start the hormones churning so early? Wouldn't it have been better if He'd planned the human sex drive to kick in when we're responsible enough to use it wisely? To be honest, we want our kids to be sexually *inactive*. But in reality, God had a different idea.

The Myth of Sexual Inactivity

The notion of a teenager being "sexually inactive" is actually a contradiction in terms. God created us as biological, sexual, and gendered persons. Your child's hormones are alive and well and doing their job, making the age-appropriate physical and emotional changes that are a normal part of human growth. We frequently use the term "sexually active" to refer to teenagers who are engaging in overt sexual activity. But this choice of terminology implies that those who are not participating in sexual behaviors are sexually *inactive*. How far from the truth! To exist, to be alive, and to relate to others is to be a sexually active person.

To label our teens as "sexually inactive" desexualizes

them. In a strange way, it's like treating them as disembodied spirits. Those who practice abstinence live in bodies that are just as sexually active as those who act out sexual impulses. All young people have sexual desires, are sexually responsive and sexually alive. Hormones attest to this. So instead of praying that God take their sex drive away, we must affirm the God-given sexuality within them and at the same time help them make responsible choices about their sexual behavior. And above all, we must be able to talk about sex and love in a way that makes sense to them.

Obviously, guiding your children in the area of sexuality is not as easy as it sounds. Is it possible to reach them, especially after they've been sexually involved with a partner? Why is sex such an awkward and embarrassing topic? Most likely you grew up with the idea that sex is a private matter and not to be talked about. You probably learned about sex like we did, from friends or older siblings with a nudge, a wink, and a giggle. How on earth do you overcome these inhibitions so you can get through to your kids?

Keeping the Secret

Recently, on a national talk show, a 13-year-old confessed that she had engaged in sexual intercourse with three different partners without using protection. When asked if her parents knew, she said, "They told me I'd better not 'go to bed with anybody' but they never asked questions while I was actually dating. I guess they just assumed we wouldn't have sex. My parents never told me much about sex and I really didn't know the first thing about it. To tell the truth, it felt really bad the first time I had sex. But, I was in love and I thought this is how you expressed it."

So many teens have gotten into trouble with sex because they lacked a responsible, informed adult to give them information and instruction. I remember how surprised I was at eight years of age when my 12-year-old sister told me where babies came from. The most amazing part for me was to learn that *my* parents had sex to have me! Trying to put this idea together with my preconceived notions about their life behind bedroom doors took quite a leap.

I'd always been comforted by the affection they had for each other and loved listening to their muffled voices in the night after we'd gone to bed. Now, the sounds I heard behind their bedroom door took on a new meaning. Thinking of them in the context of sexuality certainly expanded my view of them, but it also confused me because they never talked to any of us kids about this hidden part of their lives.

One day my younger brother and I went searching through my parent's bedroom drawers, trying to find evidence of the unspoken. Lo and behold, we found a condom that verified my sister's revelation. My brother did what any normal 8-year-old boy would do: he blew the condom up like a big balloon until it finally popped! We were really scared now, for surely we'd be reprimanded for doing something we shouldn't know anything about. But strangely enough, nothing was ever said about it. It only confirmed to us that sex should not be talked about and should remain hidden, like a condom in a drawer.

Can it be that we keep sex a mystery because it's difficult to reveal or explain this very human part of ourselves to our children? Let's face it: sex involves a loss of control, a mutual vulnerability, an expression of unbridled joy and pleasure. And for many of us, sex—even in marriage—also involves a little bit of embarrassment. Perhaps we don't want to admit to our children that we have sexual needs and desires. Perhaps we still feel a sense of guilt for enjoying a physical relationship, even though we're married. So we play the parent role. Our teenagers never hear us talk about the sexual in ourselves or our marriage because it would be a revelation about us that is too public. Keeping our sexual selves private adds to the discomfort between parents and teenagers and the inability to talk freely about the hormones stirring up in their bodies. As long as we remain remote and nonsexual, they can't imagine that we have anything important to say about the sexual sensations they're experiencing.

The secret we keep from our children grows in significance as they become curious teenagers. They must compose their ideas about sex through the clouded bits of information and misinformation they get from less reliable sources. But worse than that, they may view sexual experimentation as a sure way to learn more about their sexual selves. Perhaps your teenagers haven't received the necessary information and encouragement and have struck out on their own into uncharted sexual waters. Or perhaps you've done your best to guide them but they have chosen their own way. In either case, it's time to open up the doors of communication even further to keep your child from making more costly mistakes.

A Secret Worth Sharing

Before you do something about your teenager's activities, you need to do something for yourself. Begin by asking yourself, "What's so terrible about sex that I can't talk to my child about it?" Is it too difficult to admit that God created you with sexual desire, that you enjoy the sexual relationship with your spouse, that conceiving children is a pleasurable experience? Never be intimidated by your teenager's sexual zeal; you have more experience and know a great deal more about mature, passionate sex than they do. Sex is a bold expression of marital love that is built on emotional intimacy and committed love. You are the best one to tell your teens about the rightful connection between sex and love.

Even if your conversations with your child about sex haven't been plentiful, you and your spouse have already modeled sexuality to your children in plenty of nonverbal ways. Emotional intimacy seen in the context of a committed relationship makes an indelible impression on your teens. What unspoken messages about sexuality are you and your spouse sending to your children? Once we believe that sexuality is a secret that must be shared, we'll be able to help our teens rightly understand the great blessings of sexual intimacy in the marital relationship.

Parents Are Hurting Too

This is all good and well, you may be thinking. But we parents don't always have our lives *that* together! Each of us comes to this topic with our own sexual baggage; none of us has escaped distortions in how we think and feel about sex. And we've all made mistakes in our own journey toward sexual wholeness. When it comes right down to it, most of us will admit we haven't done such a good job in parenting our kids about sexual matters! You may feel responsible for your teenagers' sexual mistakes. You may condemn yourself for not having a better relationship with them, for being too lenient or too rigid, for being too proud or judgmental, for not understanding their struggles. You may lament the sexual mistakes of your past that have inhibited your ability to guide your children.

Let's be honest: we all fail our children in this area! Not one of us is completely successful at teaching our teenagers about sexuality. Our parents failed us and we will fail our children. *No parent is perfect!* In fact, there are circumstances in every one of our lives that have interfered with our best intentions to be a good parent. Many times our emotional, physical, or mental capacity will be overtaxed and we won't be able to give our kids what they need. Some of you have gone through painful divorce, the death of a spouse, physical or mental illness, alcoholism in the home, and so on. You may be having difficulties in your sexual relationship, or you may be grappling with sexual abuse in your past. There have been circumstances in your life that will make it especially hard for you to help your teens in their sexual struggles. You'd do anything to start over again, but it's too late for that.

You must come to the point where you can honestly say you've done the best you could under your particular circumstances. Sometimes it hasn't been enough for what your children need. But you're human—don't expect more from yourself than your best.

Who Cares for Us?

When we're hurting over the sexual indiscretions in our children's lives, we often have no place to go with our concerns. We ache over the disheartening sexual decisions our teenagers make, whether its using "900" phone numbers, watching x-rated videos or movies, sneaking out late at night to sleep with a girlfriend or boyfriend, or going through an abortion without our knowledge. We despair that as hard as we've tried, our children wouldn't listen. So we stand alone, tormented and helpless on the sidelines, watching them suffer the painful consequences of their sexual choices.

We keep our feelings of anguish and shame inside because there's no one we can confide in about this taboo topic. We even hesitate to tell our closest friends that our son is living with his girlfriend or that our daughter is pregnant before the wedding. It's comforting to know that God understands how we hurt down in our hearts for our children. But we also need help from someone who will come alongside and support us during these times.

Why This Book?

We want to come alongside you in your pain. It's time the topic of teenage sexuality be discussed in a realistic and compassionate manner. Our commitment is to deal with what *is* rather than what *should* be. This book is for parents of teenagers, ages 12 to 21, who have been sexually involved. It's our belief that many Christian teens are making less than ideal choices in their sexual behaviors, and parents need some guidance about how to help them regain a healthy sexuality.

This hasn't been an easy book to write. Whatever we say, we are likely to offend some of you. We respect the fact that each of you has a personal sexual value system that is sacred to you, and we acknowledge and honor that value system. Sometimes we'll express opinions that will be disagreeable or uncomfortable to you. We hope you'll find it a worthwhile adventure to let this be an opportunity to examine your values. In some cases, you'll be more convinced about your views and gain renewed confidence in approaching your teenagers with your values. There may be times when you'll alter or expand your thinking because you've learned something new that will help you relate to your teenager more effectively.

We believe that you can deal with the complex topic of sexuality in a way that draws your teenagers into a closer harmony with God's Word. However, even when you take responsibility for teaching, guiding, and helping your children grow in sexually healthy ways, influences outside your home will continue to impact them. They may still choose to go their own way, and you can't prevent that from happening. This book will give you an understanding of the sexual wilderness our teenagers live in. We're hopeful that some of the principles we advocate will give you and your teenager a morality of sex and love that is biblically based. We pray that the Christian values presented in this book will lead you into a relationship with your teenagers that is healthy, balanced, and whole.

2

The Day of Discovery: Facing the Truth

Alex and Norma Dickenson were concerned when a number of boys showed a great deal of interest in their attractive, shapely daughter. If there wasn't a boy calling on the phone, there was one at the front door asking for her. They were quite relieved the day she started going steady with Steve, a Christian boy from their church. Although somewhat apprehensive about her dating steadily at such a young age, at least it ended the constant stream of pursuers.

After a year, the Dickensons questioned the amount of time Steve and Paula spent together, but assured themselves that their kids were committed to sexual abstinence before marriage. The day Alex came home and found them stark naked in bed together was quite a shock, to put it mildly. He yelled at Steve to get his clothes on and leave the house immediately.

Later, Paula tried to explain to her parents, through

embarrassment and tears, that they never meant to go that far. They got carried away in the heat of watching a provocative movie on TV. The erotic feelings were like electrical currents passing through their bodies that they couldn't control. There had been other times they had been pretty far along, Paula admitted, but this was the first time they had gone all the way.

The actual discovery that our kids are having sex is a shocking event! It shakes us right out of our denial, and creates an atmosphere thick with tension and stress. Sometimes overwhelming feelings and heated words can exacerbate the problem so much that it becomes impossible to deal with. Let's take a few moments now to understand the stress we feel as parents on the day of discovery.

Three Components of Stress

When you face moments of serious stress, like discovering your child is sexually active, you not only have to deal with the event itself; you also must deal with how you as a parent perceive the situation and respond to it. Your teenager's behavior is what precipitates your stress. But it's the *combination* of these three components—the *event,* your *perception,* and the *resources* that you use to respond—that impacts your ability to handle the stress.

Think back to the day of discovery in your family— the day your teenager's sexual activities came to light. What were the actual events? In your perception, what aspects did you find hardest to deal with? What you believe about the experience is what most affects the amount of stress you experience. Furthermore, what you tell yourself about your child's behavior is tempered by the *context* of the situation.

Let's compare the following two scenarios. (1) You learn that your 22-year-old son is having sex with the woman he plans to marry in a month. (2) You find out that your 16-year-old son is having sex with his 14-year-old girlfriend. What is your response to each situation? Without condoning the behavior of either son or changing your beliefs about premarital sex, the two events cannot be dealt with in the same way. The context must be taken into account.

Your standards of judgment in each situation will influence your perception and the level of stress you reach. Even though you may believe your 22-year-old's decision is unwise, you may find it understandable. You may even believe it's permissible because you believe and trust your son will follow through on his promise to marry and support his wife and any future children they have.

In the case of your 16-year-old son, however, there are many more objectionable factors that contribute to your level of stress. For one thing, his girlfriend is a minor. Having intercourse with her is illegal, and your son could be charged with statutory rape. An unplanned pregnancy is another grave concern, since this couple is not prepared to support a child. It's not just a matter of making an unwise decision; the behavior of these two teenagers is downright irresponsible. The lives of these two young people are at risk, for neither of them is psychologically prepared for the consequences of their actions.

The level of stress you experience corresponds to your

perception of the event. If, for example, you don't believe there's anything wrong with engaged couples having sexual intercourse, the discovery will have a minimal impact. On the other hand, if you view premarital sex as an unforgivable sin no matter what the circumstances, you'll experience more stress over this situation.

All of us have *resources*, both within ourselves and in our homes and communities, that we draw on when stressed. Your resources differ from other parents and even from your spouse. They also vary in effectiveness depending on the situation. Let's examine two sets of parents coping with a similar event: their 19-year-old son is having sexual intercourse with his 18-year-old girlfriend.

Shirley and Steve Smith have a warm, honest relationship with their son, Spike. They're also close to his girlfriend, Susan, who he's been dating steadily for more than a year. Shirley relates well to Susan and accepts her into the family like a daughter. The Smiths have many good friends at church, where they've been part of a couple's support group for several years. In fact, participation in this group has been a tremendous resource to them in improving their marital relationship.

This is the first place they come to talk about their son's sexual behavior. They've discovered over the years that people in this group listen without condemnation, offer support and encouragement, and keep confidentiality. One couple that had gone through a similar situation three years earlier was particularly helpful as the Smiths revealed their distress about the situation. In this group, they could be vulnerable, deal with their feelings, and begin thinking about what they might do about the problem.

Darrall and Jamie Jones, on the other hand, have a cool, distant relationship with their son, Curt. Darrall's job frequently takes him away from home, so he's not been around for many of the important events in Curt's life. Although Jamie has sought to become friends with Curt's girlfriend, Alison, her approaches have been resisted. Most of Darrall's friends are with the business and Jamie's friends are women from church. Neither feels comfortable enough in these relationships to share their concern about their son and his girlfriend. They are left without help or hope in their distress.

The advantage the Smiths have over the Joneses should be obvious. The solid relationship the Smiths have with their son is a strength that allows for an open discussion. Their loving relationship with Susan makes it easy to talk to her with genuine concern. Knowing the teens well means they can affirm their commendable qualities as well as confront their behavior. The Smiths' personal resources and strengths help them take a proactive approach to problem solving.

Unfortunately, the Joneses lack some important resources as individuals, as a couple, and as parents. They are neither emotionally connected with nor do they communicate with their son and his girlfriend. Their marriage relationship suffers when Darrall blames the problem on his wife for not raising their kids right, and she blames him for being an absentee father. Their son, Curt, is closed and defensive when his parents approach him because he has found the love and nurture from Alison that he's lacking from his parents. Talking to separate friends only splits Darrall and Jamie further since they have no outside support system they can access together. The stress of the situation escalates through reactivity and mutual blame, worsening the situation for everyone.

Step by Step Coping

Now that you understand the components of stress, let's look at the barrage of emotional feelings you may have experienced over the loss of your teenager's virginity. *Denial* may have helped you suppress those emotions. In addition, the initial *shock* of finding out the truth may have left you feeling numb for a while. As soon as the numbness wore off, though, a number of strong emotions probably arose. The *anger* you expressed was induced by feelings of anxiety, betrayal, hurt, disappointment, and fear. After the initial fury, you may have found that discouragement and hopelessness emerged in the form of *sadness.* The loss of innocence is something for you to grieve. Eventually *acceptance* comes, allowing you to work with your teenagers toward solutions.

Although these are typical responses all parents go through, some of you will pass rapidly through one step while others may get "stuck" in another. Sometimes you'll feel overwhelmed by many emotions at once and at other times you may feel nothing. Once in a while the steps reverse themselves, or you may go back to a step that was skipped over earlier. Whatever your reactions, be patient with yourself as you go step by step through the process of feelings. We'll describe these steps in detail to help you identify the process in more concrete terms.

Denial

Denial is a mechanism which allows you to defend yourself from truth you can't accept. Continual refusal to accept the truth of your teenager's sexual behavior is psychologically exhausting! Discovery brings you to your senses; now you are forced into *seeing* rather than denying reality. And when you have consciously denied what you unconsciously suspect, you may actually feel relieved when the truth finally comes out.

Shock

When you're out of touch or in strong denial, you'll experience a high degree of shock when you discover the truth. Sometimes teens may become sexually active in an unconscious attempt to get their parents' attention. They usually feel guilty for deceiving you and may drop hints in order to be found out. Uncovering the truth will give you an opportunity to reassess your relationship with your teenagers and work toward solutions with them.

Betrayal

It hurts deeply when your children lie to you, disguise their motives, and hide their thoughts and activities. You respond in hurt and anger: "How could you do this to us?" "You're killing me with your rebellious ways!" "We've taught you the right way and you just turn your back on it." The betrayal you feel has to do with broken trust. You

feel that you've been double-crossed after sacrificing to
raise them right.

While these reactions are understandable, you must
ask hard questions of yourself when you learn you've been
deceived by your teenager. You may want to ask, "Have we
paid enough attention? Are we so busy with our lives that
we can't be bothered by theirs? Do they come and go with
little emotional connection with us? Have our rules been
so tight and inflexible that they can't dialogue with us? Do
we come down too harshly when there's an infraction of
the rules?" These personal questions can help you identify
problem areas in your relationship with your teenagers.

Anger

It's natural for you to feel angry when your teenager
acts out in sexually irresponsible ways. Anger is your signal
that something is wrong and change is needed. You may
initially blame your child or the sexual partner as the
source of your anger. But at a deeper level you really may
be angry at yourself or your spouse for failing to prevent
your child's moral failure.

When you think about anger as a personal emotion,
you're more inclined to remember that it's *your* feeling and
no one else put it there. Even though your teen's behavior
may trigger the feelings, you are responsible for the anger
and how you express it. Instead of alienating your
teenagers with rage, use the feelings as an impetus to deal
with the real issues between you. The intended goal is to
reestablish a trusting relationship between yourself and
your teenager.

Sadness

Feeling sad about what has happened leaves you in a state of low emotional energy. You've dealt with the denial and betrayal, felt the anger, and now it's time to grieve. This personal response helps you admit what's been lost so you can eventually take future action. You can get bogged down in the sad feelings, however, by telling yourself, "What's the use? I've tried to teach my kids Christian values but it doesn't do any good," or "My child's life is destroyed!" or "I must be the worst parent in the world." These negative and exaggerated messages only make things worse. Indulging in a "pity party" leaves you with a helpless, hopeless feeling that expresses itself in shaming and blaming messages.

Shaming

"Shame on you!" is an implicit or explicit message we give kids when we try to help them develop a conscience. Whereas a small dose of shame may lead to appropriate behavioral change, a persistent, self-effacing shame eats away at a person's self-worth. Harsh scrutiny and condemnation gives kids the desperate feeling in the pit of their stomach that there's something profoundly wrong with them. This crippling message soon becomes a self-fulfilling prophesy, and they begin to live up to the negative expectations you put on them.

I often hear distressing stories from clients who come out of shaming families. Paul was a grown man when he first began dealing with his father's demeaning messages and unwarranted rage. He was full of emotion as he recalled the following teenage memory:

> My father was a truck driver, so he was not home very often. When he was home, he was a tyrant, and I started wishing he'd stay away and never come back. I was so lonely and wanted to be accepted by my peers. One night a carload of friends dropped me off after a school party. We were a bit boisterous, I admit. Then, before I got out of the car, one of the girls gave me a long kiss and I was happy as a lark when I came bounding in the house. That wonderful feeling didn't last for long! My Dad had been watching from the upstairs window, and when I stepped inside the house, he was waiting for me with his rage and a strap. What had I done wrong, I wanted to know? He proceeded to accuse me of all kinds of things I hadn't done and said he was ashamed of me. I couldn't believe his response. I was thrilled to be with my friends that night and happy that one of the girls liked me. But all my father could see is what he thought I was doing, and he belted me for "not knowing any better!" The truth is he never guided me, he never told me anything about girls, he never helped me learn how to be a man. I hated him that night as I felt the pain of the belt and the sting of tears on my face. I hadn't done anything wrong. I wasn't drunk, I hadn't done drugs, I hadn't even been sexually inappropriate with a girl. But he could only think the worst of me!

Paul literally shook with terror as he recalled this humiliating night. All he ever wanted was his father's guidance and approval, but all he got was a shaming message that wounded him deep in his soul. His father's anger was unjustified, yet Paul was the one who suffered the ramifications of his father's shaming messages.

The relentless message of shame is often carried down from generation to generation, rupturing love and trust between family members. If you grew up in a home where you were shamed, you probably tend to shame your children. It takes time to heal the internal wounds of a shaming system.

We need to help our teenagers recognize right from wrong so they regret mistakes that are inconsistent with their moral values and have the strength to correct them. We want them to have integrity and a positive feeling about themselves as they make amends. If our approach shames them and motivates them to conceal or pretend, they may feel worthless and unforgivable. When we show compassion toward them, we let them know that human limitations are understandable and correctable. We want them to be able to right the wrong with a strong sense of self-worth.

Blaming

Blame is a close kinsman to shame. We can look as far back as the Adam and Eve account and see how it works. When God asks Adam and Eve why they are hiding themselves, the first thing they do is place blame on someone else. In fact, Adam actually blames God for giving him the woman who has caused him to sin. Eve, as you know, blames the serpent. "The Devil made me do it" mentality is alive and well in our world today. It's not only our teens who point the finger at someone else to cover up their own mistakes; we do it, too. Parents blame each other when teenagers are in trouble. You may say to your spouse, "If only *you* had been more firm in child rearing," or "This wouldn't have happened if *you* paid more attention to Richy," or "*You* kept putting off the sex talk *you* were supposed to have with Sue."

Blaming gets you nowhere because it keeps you from looking at yourself and your role in the issue. Instead of blaming or shaming your kids and spouse about what you've discovered, look deeper into yourself. Take personal responsibility for what is your fault. Then draw on the inner strength God gives to forge ahead.

Acceptance at Last

Only when you've looked the truth straight in the eye and accepted the reality of your child's sexual activities can you go forward. Acceptance brings an emotional stability to the situation that allows you to finally deal with the matter at hand. You're reading this book because you've dealt with your emotional reactions in a sufficient and appropriate way and now you're ready for proactive steps. We close with a few guidelines to help you get started on the road to recovery with your teenager.

1. A simple rule of thumb is to honestly acknowledge your feelings and concern by beginning with an "I" message along with a feeling word and a statement of the problem. For example,

> "*I'm angry* that you've *been sleeping with your boyfriend,*" or "*I'm sad to learn you've been having intercourse with your girlfriend.*"

2. Next, let your teen know how the event effects your parent-child relationship.

> "It's *put a strain* on our relationship and I'm having trouble knowing *how to interact with you about this.*"

3. Now follow up that statement with what you'd like to happen—your wishes or needs.

> "I'd *like* us to talk about what happened so we can *find a solution.*"

4. Let your teenager know you will listen. You may also need to ask forgiveness for some of your earlier reactions.

> "I want to make it safe for you to talk honestly, so that I can understand how you think and feel about what's happened. *I'm sorry* I lost my cool last night. I know it didn't help matters. But I want you to talk freely and *I want to listen to what you have to say.*"

5. Work together to set the goals and find the solutions to the problem.

> "*We* need to find a solution that is acceptable to your mother/father and I and one you'll agree to follow."

You, the parent, are clearly responsible for making the final decision about what's acceptable. But unless it's done in collaboration with your teenager, it's highly unlikely that they'll keep their end of the bargain.

6. Make a contract and establish ways to monitor it.

"Here's our *agreement.* I've included what we agreed to as parents, and what you've agreed to do. We'll meet weekly to see that we're keeping our commitments to each other. Then, after three months, we'll review how it's going so we can make changes if needed."

This contract clearly states the agreed-upon commitments made between you and your teenager. It clarifies the terms and keeps you accountable to each other for what's written in the contract. It's important to include what teenagers want their parents to do, such as asking permission before entering their room, treating their friends with more respect, or being less rigid about a certain rule. This gives them a chance to express what they need from us as well as what we need from them. Signing the contract makes it more official. Review the contract after a certain length of time so you can renegotiate if necessary.

When you made the traumatic discovery that your child was having sex, you, like most people, probably reacted first and thought about it later. In this chapter, we've shown how your reactions to discovering your teenager's sexual intimacy vary according to the event, your perception of the event, and the resources you bring to the situation. We've presented a step-by-step process for dealing with the emotional feelings that accompany discovery. We've offered some specific guidelines to help you get started toward a solution. We realize it won't be quite so simple and straightforward as it looks on paper. But the stages and principles should give you an understanding of the process you are going through in this difficult time.

3

What Every Parent and Teen Should Know

Okay, you just got hit with the news. Your suspicions were confirmed. You've moved from denial to acceptance. Now what? The most important thing you can do right now is to make sure your son or daughter clearly understands the consequences of teenage sexual intercourse in this turbulent period of our social history.

Your teenagers are engaging in life-and-death behaviors. In regard to life, they need to know the complete facts about conception and contraception. In regard to death, they need to know how to prevent life-threatening sexually transmitted diseases that can impair their lives as well as the lives of their unborn children.

Teaching Chastity is Not Enough

The recent trend of having young people take a vow of virginity is one method of keeping them chaste. The

intent of the "purity pledge" is to help them see that "true
love waits." Signing the pledge en masse can be a powerful
way for thousands of teenagers to join together to affirm
this stance. The symbolic acts of wearing a ring, writing a
sealed letter to a future spouse, or signing a pledge card can
give them strength to keep their commitment to chastity.

But, as those of you who are dealing with sexually
involved teenagers know, this is not enough! In fact,
sometimes the very vows they make before God and their
parents may put them in a bind when it comes to taking
responsible precautions later in life. A vow is promise that
sometimes binds them to unfortunate consequences.

Christian young people are especially prone to engage
in *unprotected* sex because they can't admit to doing
something that is incongruent with their Christian beliefs.
When the moment of temptation comes, they're unpre-
pared. Because they'd made a promise to be chaste, they
never seriously considered that they might someday break
that promise.

Spreading the message of chastity is something we
clearly applaud. But let's teach safe sex along with this
message. Vows get broken whether they're made by adults
or teenagers, and they're insufficient in and of themselves
to keep teenagers chaste. A vow to follow God's way is a
good thing, but we need more! This is the very reason
Jesus came into the world, to bring redemption when we
fail to keep our vows.

Several years ago Jack was speaking on the topic of
adolescent sexuality to a group of parents of high schoolers. After the presentation, a parent confronted him about
the statement he made that many young people will

engage in sexual intercourse regardless of what parents say. This father was particularly offended by Jack's suggestion that teenagers need to be informed about birth control. The parent was adamant about his belief that teaching birth control techniques to a teenager is "just an invitation for them to go hog-wild."

This attitude must be openly challenged. Underlying such a statement is the assumption that giving contraception information undoubtedly leads to premarital sex and that keeping adolescents ignorant keeps them chaste. These conclusions are not supported by the evidence. The far greater concern is that lack of information places teens in high risk of unwanted pregnancy and exposure to sexually transmitted diseases.

The message of abstinence must be emphasized and encouraged as a valuable way for teenagers to conduct their lives. A certain number of teens, however, will still engage in sex no matter how much we hope they'll remain virgins. Since this is the case, we must give them information on pregnancy and sexual disease prevention. This is your responsibility as a parent, for if you neglect to provide this information, you run the risk of failing your son or daughter on a life-and-death matter.

The Risk of Ignorance vs. Information

Teenagers learn about sex even when parents are not the teachers. There are few topics teenagers are more interested in; it's a central aspect of their development. But where do they get their information and how accurate is it? Needless to say, the information passed on from teenager to teenager is a combination of sense and nonsense. Since admitting ignorance of sexual matters would result in a loss of status in the eyes of their peers, adolescents are apt to agree with just about anything and pass it along as fact. The typical teenager's knowledge of sexuality is woefully inadequate, full of erroneous beliefs, myths, and misconceptions. What they need is accurate information so they can make informed, responsible choices.

It's quite a challenge for you, we're sure, to be told you need to provide knowledge about contraception and protection so your daughter or son can make responsible choices, especially when you want them to be celibate. But if you expect them to act responsibly about their sexual behaviors, they must be informed about the *consequences* of irresponsible behavior. One unfortunate scenario we find repeated in our counseling with teenagers is that young people engage in sex without either one taking responsibility for their actions. Here's just one story to illustrate the point.

Marcie, a quiet, plain girl was just 15 when she first met Rod. Going through the usual teenage struggles of self-worth and attractiveness, she seized the opportunity as soon as he showed an interest in her. She described it as "forever love" and determined never to let go. Rod, a gangling boy of 16, lived alone with his mother; his father had left home when Rod was just three years old. He was thrilled to have a full-time girlfriend to confide in. Things hadn't been going very well between him and his mother, and it made him feel important to have someone look up to him and see him as strong.

Marcie and Rod were inseparable; it seemed they couldn't manage life without each other. When they got on each other's nerves, they quickly made up, because they couldn't stand being on the outs. They became heavily involved sexually, and pregnancy soon followed. Neither of them was ready to care for a child, so without consulting anyone, they chose to have an abortion. Although they clung to each other through this excruciating experience, their relationship was sinking fast. They knew something was wrong but had no idea how to change. So they continued to stay lost in each other.

Things went from bad to worse. They desperately wanted intimacy, but all they had to offer each other was dependency and sex. It's absurd to think that two immature teenagers like these had any basis for developing the deeper qualities of intimacy. When Marcie began complaining about wanting something more, Rod responded out of frustration and inadequacy. He threw his hands up in the air, declaring it was impossible to please her. Neither of them knew how to achieve the kind of intimacy they longed for, and eventually their relationship crumbled.

Few teenagers are mature enough to sustain a relationship as demanding as marriage. In fact, the statistics show that eighty percent of teenage marriages end in divorce in the U.S. Yet this doesn't keep teenagers from having sex and bearing children. The story of Marcie and Rod illustrates what happens when parents remain silent. For sexually active teens, ignorance is not bliss. It results in a lack of concern for themselves, each other, the potential life of an unborn child, for family and for society at large.

It only takes two teenagers to make a baby, but it takes two teenagers *and* their parents to *keep* from making a baby or an irreversible mistake that could cost them their health or their lives.

Risking the Dangers or Taking Responsibility

It may be helpful to review some of the reasons teenagers give for failing to use protection while having sex. Common responses are:

1. We don't know what to use or how to get it.
2. We didn't plan to have sex. It just happened and we didn't have any protection.
3. We didn't really believe she'd get pregnant.
4. I secretly wanted a little baby I could love who would love me back.
5. I've fathered two children already and I'm proud of my virility.
6. Sex is more exciting when it's risky. It spoils things if we use protection.
7. I tried the pill but I put on weight. It's more trouble than it's worth.
8. If I take precautions, I have to admit to myself I premeditated having sex. That's not consistent with my Christian beliefs.

Teenagers from Christian homes are especially susceptible to this last excuse. Buying contraceptives and having them available is in direct contradiction to the decision they made, and also their parents' desires, to remain celibate. If they do have sex, it seems worse to take precautions than to deal with the incongruence between their beliefs and actions.

No matter what the reasons, when safe sex and/or celibacy are not practiced, pregnancy and disease are serious consequences. At the very least, asking our teens to be responsible for their sexual involvement helps them take a more realistic look at themselves and a reflective look at the nature of their current sexual relationship. The appeal to parents is that unless we take seriously our responsibility to inform our teenagers about contraception and disease, they will most likely not take responsibility for themselves and their actions.

Birth Control Information

In 1992, an Associated Press release announced that teen births were up for the fourth straight year. In 1990, 533,483 babies were born to mothers under 20, including 194,984 to girls 17 years and younger. The statistics are alarming, especially in light of the psychological immaturity of these young women and their sexual partners.

Birth control is the attempt to prevent conception and comes in a variety of forms. The ideal birth control method should be both effective and safe and a method agreed upon by both participants. In the case of unmarried teenagers, it would seem that a method will be the most effective when it's easy to use and is freely available.

Condom

The most common contraceptive method for males is

the *condom*, a latex rubber sheath worn tightly over the penis. The condom prevents conception by preventing sperm from reaching the vagina. Although the condom is effective when used properly, it is only 90% effective in actual use. The advantage of the condom is that it is readily available, costs under a dollar, and can be used when needed. The major disadvantage to the condom is that it is not fool-proof! Teenagers are more likely than experienced adults to be in the 10-15% margin of error that occurs when the condom is inappropriately put on, slips off, or leaks.

The AIDS epidemic has increased the popularity of the condom as the safest contraceptive for those unsure of their sex partner's former experiences. When used with a spermicide containing nonoxynol-9 or octoxynol, it provides protection against organisms that give rise to sexually transmitted diseases. Only latex condoms are effective against the AIDS virus. Oil- or petroleum-based lubricants should not be used; they can produce microscopic holes in the condom.

The Pill

The most commonly used contraceptive method for females is the *birth control pill*. Female birth control pills produce sex hormones that interfere with the normal ovulation process. When properly used, birth control pills are nearly 100% effective. While the pill may be the safest and most effective method for married persons who regularly engage in sex, a teenager who engages in sex from time to time with different partners does not protect herself from sexually transmitted disease. Teenagers may not remember to take the pill regularly, which puts them at risk. Or they may dislike some of the side effects (nausea and vomiting, fluid retention, weight gain, headaches, tenderness in breasts, and dizziness) and stop taking it. Because there are some health risks to be aware of, taking the pill must be monitored by medical professionals.

Perhaps a more realistic form of birth control for teenage girls is the *morning-after pill*, but it has not been approved for general use by the Food and Drug Administration. An injectable drug, Depo-Provera, that prevents pregnancy for three months, has recently been approved for use in the United States.

Norform implants (a small wheel placed just under the skin in a fifteen-minute surgical procedure) prevent conception for five years. The implants aren't usually available for girls under 18, but this method was recently approved in Baltimore for high school students. Maryland has one of the nation's highest teenage pregnancy rates in the U.S. While Norform has stirred some controversy among parents, it is considered to be one of the best methods of birth control for sexually active teenagers. Of course it does not protect against sexually transmitted diseases.

Other Methods of Birth Control

There are a number of contraceptive foams, creams, and jellies that a female can use to prevent conception. Most of these block entrance of sperm into the uterus and at the same time kill or immobilize the sperm. To be effective, these contraceptives need to be inserted 5 to 15 minutes prior to sexual intercourse.

An intrauterine device (IUD) can be inserted into the uterus by a physician as a means of preventing conception. When properly in place, the IUD has an effectiveness rate of 98%, but it can fall out without a woman's knowledge. There's also a possibility of infection with the IUD. Some are opposed to it for religious reasons because it prevents fertilized eggs from becoming implanted.

The diaphragm is a dome-shaped rubber cap stretched over a collapsible metal ring. It covers the cervical opening and prevents sperm from entering the uterus. The diaphragm must be fitted properly by a physician in order to be effective. Sometimes spermicidal cream or jelly is combined with the diaphragm in order to assure maximum protection against conception.

The most recent birth control innovation is the vaginal pouch or female condom. This condom was approved for use in Switzerland and France during the early part of 1992. It has been approved for use in the United States, and preliminary tests indicate it's a simple and safe means of birth control and disease prevention.

The Risks of Sexually Transmitted Diseases

Just before the start of the 1991-92 professional basketball season, the sports world was stunned by Magic Johnson's announcement that he was retiring from basketball because he had tested positive for HIV (Human Immunodeficiency Virus), the cause of AIDS. Shortly thereafter, Magic began evangelizing for "safe sex." Besides drawing attention to the fact that engaging in sexual intercourse can lead to death, it helped raise the issue of what "safe sex" means.

The modern term *sexually transmitted disease* (STD) replaced the old term, *venereal disease* (VD). These are bacterial and viral diseases which are primarily passed on from person to person through sexual intercourse. Acquired immune deficiency syndrome (AIDS) is only one of many sexually transmitted diseases that have long-term, dangerous, chronic physical debilitations.

Although only 1% of HIV/AIDS victims in the United States are adolescents, 20% of all persons with AIDS are in their 20s. Because of the average 8 to 11-year latency period between HIV infection and the onset of AIDS, it would not be an exaggeration to estimate that at least 40,000 present AIDS victims were infected *during* adolescence. The number of teenagers diagnosed with AIDS has recently increased by forty-three percent.

In terms of numbers, AIDS is just the tip of a large and lethal iceberg. Two and a half million American teenagers (or 20% of all Americans) are infected with some type of sexually transmitted disease each year. Approximately one out of every six sexually active adolescents has contracted a sexually transmitted disease. It is estimated that only half of American high school students who engage in sexual intercourse use adequate protection.

Bacterial Communicable Diseases

Although many forms of bacteria are harmless, several

types can cause illness when they take up residence in the human body. Bacterial diseases spread through sexual contact are like any other bacterial infection: they can be treated successfully with antibiotics if they are discovered early.

Gonorrhea is the most common bacteria-based sexually transmitted disease, infecting 2 million people every year. In men, the symptoms of gonorrhea appear within several days following contact in the form of a puss-like discharge from the penis or a burning sensation during urination. The symptoms can either be intense or so slight that a man is unaware that he has been infected. In fact, the reason gonorrhea is so prevalent is because it often goes unnoticed until the infected person has spread the disease to other sexual partners. Gonorrhea can be effectively treated and cured with penicillin. When left untreated, however, it moves through other parts of both the male and female reproductive systems, causing sterility in extreme cases.

Syphilis, also referred to as "pox," "scab," or "Spanish sickness," is less common than gonorrhea, but its effects are more harmful. After contact, syphilis takes several weeks to several months before appearing in the form of sores on the genitals, lips, or inside the mouth. Although the surface sores may heal in several weeks, the disease will spread throughout the body by way of the bloodstream if not treated.

The second-stage symptoms of syphilis will show themselves in the form of a fever, rash, genital warts, or pain in the joints. For most people, the disease ends several months after the appearance of these symptoms, even without treatment. Among approximately one-third of the untreated cases, however, the disease continues quietly over a period of years until the heart or the central nervous system begins to deteriorate. Due to the practice of regular medical examinations which include blood tests, this third-stage syphilis is very rare today. Once detected, syphilis can be cured with antibiotics.

Chlamydia is a disease rapidly spreading among college students today. Although chlamydia may be considered a mild form of gonorrhea, antibiotics other than penicillin must be used to successfully treat it. The disease may lead to other serious health problems such as PID (Pelvic Inflammatory Disease).

Viral Communicable Diseases

Unlike invading bacteria, a virus can only be seen under a microscope. More alarming is the fact that there is no successful way to treat a virus. Like the common cold, a viral sexual infection is incurable, placing victims in the position of needing to recover without the help of medicine.

Herpes is a name for a family of viruses which include strains such as chicken pox, shingles, and mononucleosis. There are two variations of the common strain, *herpes simplex.* Type 1 herpes shows itself in the form of fever blisters and cold sores around the mouth. Infection of Type 1 herpes can be spread through kissing or oral-genital contact. Type 2 herpes is generally referred to as genital herpes because it causes painful sores and blisters in the genitals, buttocks, and thighs.

Once a person comes into contact with the herpes virus, it takes several days to several weeks for the first symptoms to appear. The affected areas of skin itch and eventually form sores or blisters, accompanied by fatigue, fever, or achiness. The most contagious period occurs when the sores and blisters erupt, releasing millions of viruses ready to find a new home. Once the sores form scabs, the contagious period is greatly reduced. After the sores have healed, the virus usually subsides with little or no permanent damage, reappearing periodically in the form of blisters and sores. In a few more severe cases, however, herpes may appear to be dormant but travel to the brain, spinal cord, or the eyes, causing serious damage.

The good news about herpes is that over time the reoccurring symptoms becomes less frequent and less bothersome. The bad news is that there is no effective cure; one may have to live with the virus within one's body for life. Although the physical effects of herpes may be minimal, the psychological effect of not being able to rid oneself of the disease may be more serious. Herpes carriers can undergo periods of depression and despair because they have no control over the disease.

Mononucleosis is popularly known as "the kissing disease," because it results from a virus which is transmitted orally. Among young people, the major symptoms of mononucleosis are sleepiness, accompanied by a sore throat, mild fever, fatigue, and an achy feeling. "Mono" requires weeks and sometimes months of rest.

Genital warts are growths near the genital or anal areas that are caused by a sexually transmitted virus. Although they are usually painless and of minor consequence, they may contribute to cervical and genital cancer. For this reason, these warts need to be diagnosed and removed by a medical professional. Genital warts appear to be contagious as long as they are present on the body.

Hepatitis is a liver disease which can be sexually transmitted. Hepatitis A is usually transmitted only where there is contact with the anus. Hepatitis B can be transmitted in a variety of ways because the virus lives in saliva, blood, semen, vaginal fluids, and sweat. The symptoms of Hepatitis A are usually minor—nausea, fatigue, achiness, fever, and a tender liver. But Hepatitis B lasts much longer and may result in jaundice. Rest, a proper diet, and eliminating alcohol and cigarettes usually defeats the virus within a few months.

Acquired Immune Deficiency Syndrome

A handful of AIDS cases began to appear in the United States in the early 1980s. Federal officials at the Center For Disease Control estimate that today over one million Americans are infected with the human immuno-deficiency virus (HIV), the virus that causes AIDS. Like most viral sexually transmitted diseases, AIDS has no known cure. It has become the most feared and most misunderstood of the sexually transmitted diseases.

As its name implies, AIDS is an infectious, transmittable disease in which the body's immune system is damaged, making a person vulnerable to a number of serious, often fatal infections and cancers. Most common are: pneumocystic pneumonia (PCP); cytomegalovirus (CMV), a condition whose symptoms may include diar-

rhea, retinitis, and blindness; thrush (Candidiasis), a
fungal infection; shingles (Herpes), which are painful sores
that form along the course of a nerve; and Karposi's
sarcoma, a cancer of the skin and mucous membranes.
AIDS patients ultimately die of one of these diseases
because they have no immune system to fight these
multiple infections and cancers.

Misconceptions abound about how AIDS is transmitted. The AIDS virus lives within the blood, semen, and
other body fluids. As such, the virus can only be
transmitted if fluid from an infected person is taken
directly into another person's body. Although the disease
is spreading rampantly, the ways in which it can be
transmitted are really quite limited.

• *Blood Contamination.* AIDS can be transmitted to
people receiving transfusions of HIV-infected blood and
blood products; to intravenous drug abusers who share
needles; and to health care workers who are accidentally
exposed to HIV-infected blood that enters their bodies
through breaks in their skin.

• *Sexual Contact.* AIDS can be transmitted through
homosexual and heterosexual encounters with someone
who has AIDS or HIV.

• *Perinatal Contact.* An HIV-infected mother can
transmit the virus to her unborn child through blood
exchanges and also to her baby through HIV-infected
breast milk.

The virus *cannot* be transmitted through a sneeze, a
cough, drinking from a used glass, or touching an object an
AIDS carrier has touched. The two most common ways

the AIDS virus is transmitted are through anal and vaginal intercourse and by using a hypodermic needle that has previously been used by an infected carrier. Transmission through oral-genital sex, when abrasions are involved, is less common but can occur.

The symptoms of AIDS during its early stage include weight loss, skin growths and rashes, swollen glands, and fever. In its advanced stage, AIDS patients can suffer from mental and neurological problems such as forgetfulness, impaired speech, tremors, and seizures. AIDS-infected patients suffer excruciatingly painful deaths.

The issue of AIDS testing is frequently met with outcries over civil rights and personal freedom violations. But we highly recommend that anyone who chooses to be sexually involved should be willing to be tested and to ask their sexual partner to be tested as well. The Eliza test is the principle screening test for HIV. If someone has a positive Eliza, then the test should be repeated for certainty. If the results are still positive, the Western Blot, a more sensitive and sophisticated test, is performed. At this point an individual is diagnosed as HIV-positive. This does not mean the person has AIDS, but he or she may get AIDS sometime in the future. Nearly everyone who contracts HIV develops AIDS within ten years. The length of time between infection and the development of AIDS symptoms, anywhere from five to eight years, makes it hard to detect where and when a person might have contracted the disease. Once AIDS symptoms have begun in earnest, death follows in about two years.

AIDS is approaching epidemic proportions in cultures around the world through promiscuous sex and the sharing of drug needles. It affects both homosexuals and heterosexuals alike, although statistics are still highest among the homosexual population. The more sexually promiscuous, the greater the chances of unknowingly being infected by HIV.

It is vital that your children know the facts about AIDS and other sexually communicable diseases. You might approach the topic by reading a novel or biography of an AIDS person, or watching TV programs showing the personal impact of HIV/AIDS. Learn the facts and figures of the epidemic. Visit a health care unit or community organization that works with people infected with HIV or developed AIDS. Discuss safe sex practices and birth control with your teens, and encourage the youth workers at your church to plan youth group discussions on the topic.

Mature Enough To Practice Responsible Sex?

You might be wondering at this point whether your teenagers are mature enough to manage their sexual feelings in a responsible way. In an article entitled, "Managing Sexual Feelings in the Christian Community," Dean Kleiver offers three sources for evaluating adolescent maturity: (1) evidence from overt and observable behavior; (2) evidence from thinking and attitudes; and (3) evidence from feelings and how the child deals with them. Here are some guidelines for evaluating your teenager's maturity level.

Evidence from overt behavior. Do your children demonstrate the ability to keep their promises? Are their actions consistent with the values they express? Do they ever ridicule friends' values or urge them to go beyond their limits? Teenagers who follow through on promises show that they are able to live within their own limits. And setting limits is what responsible sex is all about. But living within our own limits is not enough; maturity involves respecting our partner's limits, too.

Evidence from thinking and attitudes. Do your teenagers think before they act? Do they talk about the reasons behind their actions? Does their reasoning indicate some original thought or do they just adopt the attitudes they see on TV or hear from their friends? If your teenagers think seriously about it, they'll realize they don't have all the answers regarding sex at this point in their lives. And if they don't take the time to think about the whys of sex, they'll inevitably find themselves in some difficult situations.

Evidence from responsiveness to feelings. Most teenagers don't express their deeper feelings freely with their parents. You may have a hard time figuring out exactly what your children feel about their sexuality and about how they are expressing it. Do your teens tend to hide their feelings from others as well as from you and your spouse? Do they seem uptight or ashamed when the topic of sex comes up? Are they able to empathize with others and understand their friends' feelings?

A mature approach to sexuality involves, first of all, admitting and coming to terms with our fears, our feelings of guilt, and our desires. When we acknowledge our feelings, we learn to trust them. When we trust our feelings, we can understand the meaning behind them.

Secondly, maturity means demonstrating healthy feelings about sexuality: comfortableness, vulnerability, a sense of fun, and a congruence between values and sexual activity.

Gauging whether your teenagers have sufficient maturity to manage their sexual behavior is quite a task. Many of us will have to admit that we, too, fall short on some of these points, which should be a reminder to us that we need to continue to mature throughout our lives. But taking a sexual maturity temperature gives you and your teenagers a chance to honestly evaluate their ability to make responsible choices. At the very least, it will help them recognize they have a long way to go.

It seems a shame that teenagers are in such a hurry to grow up today. As parents, we need to find ways to help them slow down, to take time to mature not only in body, but also in mind and spirit. And even though the hormones urge them on, we can help them mature in a healthy, balanced way by encouraging them to make responsible decisions that will enhance rather than endanger that growth process.

4

Love That Neither Condones nor Condemns

I love you, but I don't approve of what you've done!" This is the message we need to offer our teenagers when they've made sexual mistakes. Your children need to know they are loved as they are, not just as they behave. This is the kind of love God offers. Just as the Ten Commandments are given by the God who loves us and has a plan for a fulfilling and purposeful life, we must offer guidelines out of our loving desire for our teens to experience a wholesome, balanced, fulfilling life. And just as God offers us never-ending forgiveness when we come in repentance, so must we be ready to forgive and welcome back our wayward teens.

Unconditional love is not a wishy-washy love. It is one that is willing to confront behavior that is out of sync with biblical principles. But often we parents speak in a tone that condemns rather than empowers our teens. The delicate balance of confronting and loving may make you feel you're on an emotional tightrope with little room to maneuver. Yet it's worth the risk; the times you are honest and open with your teens are the times of greatest intimacy.

Rose Marie and her mother, Juanita, discovered this wonderful fact firsthand. At the end of a week-long family church camp, Rose Marie was convicted about her promiscuous sexual activities with several boys in school. When Juanita joined her daughter at the campfire that night, Rose Marie openly wept in her mother's arms. On their long walk back to the cabin, they talked honestly about how difficult things had gotten between them. For the first time in years, Juanita was able to offer more than angry, condemning comments about her daughter's sexual behavior. She was able to express her sadness about their inability to communicate and about the hurtful choices Rose Marie had made. Their vulnerability toward each other brought love and clarity, a balance they sorely needed.

Covenant Love As Parental Love

The Bible sets forth a clear model of parenting based on *covenant* love. In Genesis 17, God not only offered a covenant to Abraham, but asked for his participation in the covenant: "I will establish my covenant as an everlasting covenant between me and you and your descendants after you for the generations to come. . . . As for you, you must keep my covenant, you and your descendants after you for the generations to come" (vv. 7, 9). There are several lessons to learn from this passage.

First, God did not offer Abraham a choice. That is, God did not say, "Now I am going to commit myself to you *if* this is your desire." Instead, the covenant was based *entirely* on God's action. God's offer was in no way based on Abraham keeping *his* end of the bargain. In the same way, we offer our children unconditional love regardless of their response to us. You are the mature adult who is able to commit your unfailing love without strings attached.

Second, even though God desired and even commanded a response from Abraham—the rite of circumcision—this did *not* make the offer conditional. God didn't say, "I will keep my covenant *if* you and your descendants are circumcised." The covenant stood whether or not Abraham and his descendants practiced circumcision. God established a unilateral, everlasting covenant without conditions. Even when our teens reject our love, we don't break our commitment to them. We give our love without a guarantee that it will be returned—a "for-better-or-worse" proposition.

Third, the potential benefits or blessings provided by the covenant were conditional. Abraham and his descendants were given the option of benefitting from the covenant, but they would have to fulfill their end of the bargain in order to receive the blessing. In like manner, your children benefit from your commitment by responding to your love. A two-way, open relationship is their blessing. The fact that nothing they do will cause you to withdraw your love provides a secure foundation for them. Your teenagers may suffer painful consequences by turning away from the wise counsel you give. But one thing they must be sure of is that you will love them forever.

Fourth, God extended the covenant to continuing generations of family members even though it was impossible for Abraham to anticipate or become responsible for the actions of the future descendants. The only thing he could do was to personally respond to God in the best way he knew how. It's the same for us. You cannot begin to anticipate the actions of your children or your children's children, but you can and must faithfully give them your love. God gives us free choice to respond to his love and commandments, and if our love is unconditional, we will offer the same to our teenagers.

The biblical account of God as parent is a poignant picture of persistent love and grace. The ultimate fulfillment of the covenant is Christ himself, God's supreme expression of love. 1 John 4:10 expresses it this way: "This is love; not that we loved God, but that he loved us and sent his Son as an atoning sacrifice for our sins."

The New Testament story of the prodigal son shows another compassionate picture of God as the father who welcomes a wayward son home with open arms. Like Dorothy in the Wizard of Oz or E.T., when we lose our way we desperately want to get back home. And when we do, God responds with outstretched arms. It's especially interesting to note that the father of the prodigal son made no attempt to hold his son back. Rather than stay in the safe confines of his home, the son chose to break away and do his own thing. At this point the father does an extraordinary thing: he gives his son his inheritance and lets him go! Could you do the same? Could you allow your teenager the freedom to turn from your wisdom and teaching to make his or her own mistakes?

Our natural instinct as parents is to hold on. We may even cajole, threaten, play martyr games, manipulate, or do just about anything rather than let them go their own way. Yet you know in your heart that your teenager may choose to reject your values. You may have demonstrated leadership in your home and clearly communicated your value system. You may have offered firm and loving guidelines. But in the end, your teens may choose a different way. It's heartbreaking to have your love and good intentions scorned, but you have the choice to remain steadfast in your love and leave the door open for their return.

Grace As Parental Acceptance

By its very nature, a covenant *is* grace. From a human perspective, the unconditional love of God makes no sense unless we see it in terms of grace. Grace is a relational word that means *unmerited favor*. The opposite of grace is law.

A parent-child relationship that is based on law rather than love is disastrous. When rules are the focus, your home becomes an arena of contracts and restrictions rather than one of grace and mercy. Perfection is the name of the game. And when rules are rigidly set up to govern behavior, the pressure for perfection is sure to induce shame. Failure is inevitable, and when children don't measure up they begin to feel there is something radically

wrong with them. They will look for a place to be loved
and accepted, and a sexual relationship may be that place.

Cloretta could never do anything right from the time
she learned to make her bed to the day she failed to get
straight "A's" in high school. She fell short of the
standards set by her parents, feeling inadequate and
hopeless that she would ever be a "good enough" daughter.
The only place Cloretta felt slightly good about herself was
when she was with her boyfriend. He let her know there
was something she could do right, and that was making
love. Cloretta's parents had issued plenty of rules about
dating. But since she didn't believe it was possible to live
up to her parent's expectations, Cloretta simply disregard-
ed the whole bag. In her mind, she at least was having
some good feelings about herself when she was with her
boyfriend.

When you think about it, the meaning and joy of
being a Christian would be deadened if we thought of our
relationship with God in terms of just following rules.
Obeying out of fear and shame rather than out of desire
and respect leads to legalism and creates distance between
parents and teens. But grace leads to responsible, meaningful behavior that enhances relationships.

Some of you may be resisting the idea of grace without
law, wondering if we're dismissing the need for any
guidelines in the home. Our answer is taken from Romans
10:4: "Christ is the end of the law so that there may be
righteousness for everyone who believes." It's not that the
law itself is bad, for it points the way to God. But since no
human is perfect, the law can never be fulfilled. Christ is
the "end of the law" in the sense that he is the perfect

fulfillment of the law. We are righteous not through the law, but through Christ; our salvation is through Him alone.

We believe that God's ideal is grace as a *basis* for how we relate to our teens. We agree, however, that law is necessary for proper *functioning* and responsible interaction between you and your teenagers. After all, God not only gave us the Ten Commandments but also the entire scripture as a guideline for how to live our lives in relationships. In reality, much of the daily routine of family life must be lived according to agreed-upon rules, regularity, and order. Rules are given for the sake of both parents and children. They are not used for repression or limitation, but for freedom and happiness.

When our kids were teens, Jack attempted to bolster the evidence that we could be a family of grace. He decided to rid our family of its existing contractual agreements by doing away with the list of rules we had established. Judy thought the household was functioning well under the rules we had carefully established in dialogue with the children. In his idealism, Jack suggested that we be a radically Christian family and interact with each other in a gracious, serving manner, doing away with all rules. The kids were ecstatic about the idea; Judy was the only skeptical one. Jack went on to say that our kids could decide on their own curfews and make decisions about where to go and what to do without asking permission.

Needless to say, the breakdown of this "family of grace" was swift. After a few weeks, testing the limits was at its peak. No one knew where anyone else was or when

they were coming home, since each was operating inde-
pendently. Once our teenage daughter stayed out past
midnight without phoning us. Jack was nearly beside
himself with worry, even though it was he who had given
her this freedom. That incident was the catalyst that threw
the entire family into anxiety, anger, and chaos.

This disastrous failure helped us realize that contracts
are an important part of a family of grace. They represent
clear commitments we make to each other within the
family. Contractual agreements are necessary to insure
mutual satisfaction and fairness as well as mutual respect
and consideration for each other. One interesting twist in
this experiment was that our teenagers wanted to know
where *we* were and when *we* were coming home just as
much as we needed to know about them. We quickly
learned how important it was to cooperate together in
establishing family rules so we could live together in a
smoothly run household.

Condemning the Action But Not the Person

Kids go to great lengths to hide sexual behaviors when
they think parents will disapprove of what they're doing.
The Bible offers some important instruction on how to
approach our children in matters of sexual indiscretion.
We have just suggested that *covenant love* and *grace* form
the foundation for a secure, reliable relationship with our
teenagers. Now we'll build upon this foundation by
illustrating how you can confront your child's behavior
without condemning the child.

Our example comes from John 8, an encounter

between the Pharisees and Jesus over the woman caught in adultery. The Pharisees asked Jesus to confront the woman's behavior in verse 5: "In the Law Moses commanded us to stone such women. Now what do you say?" Jesus' response provides us with a model for dealing with wrong behavior and at the same time showing compassion for the person.

> But Jesus bent down and started to write on the ground with his finger. When they kept on questioning him, he straightened up and said to them, "If any one of you is without sin, let him be the first to throw a stone at her." Again he stooped down and wrote on the ground. At this, those who heard began to go away one at a time, the older ones first, until only Jesus was left, with the woman still standing there. Jesus straightened up and asked her, "Woman, where are they? Has no one condemned you?" "No one, sir," she said. "Then neither do I condemn you," Jesus declared. "Go now and leave your life of sin." (vv. 6–11)

There are some helpful principles to be gleaned from this response. First, notice that Jesus established the fact that all persons have one thing in common—_no one is without sin._ We as parents are not without sin. We mustn't place ourselves in a superior moral position. When our children stand accused before us, they already know of their moral failure, but they know about our moral failures, too. We start at the point that we are not without sin, and come to them in an attitude of humility.

Second, Jesus did not condemn the woman but neither did he ignore her adulterous behavior. He acknowledged her behavior, along with the recognition of the sinful behaviors of her accusers. Then he immediately counseled her, "Go now and leave your life of sin."

These last two principles can be combined into one: *Condemn the sinful behavior but not the person.* Recognize that you are on common ground with your teens as sinners saved by grace. Don't condemn your teenager, but point out and declare the *behavior* as wrong. Then ask that they go and sin no more. And finally, try to encourage and empower them to change. The scripture text doesn't tell us whether the woman did as Jesus counseled, and you have no guarantee that your child will heed your counsel, either. But your compassion for your children, like Jesus' compassion for the adulterous woman, will inspire them to change and correct their behavior.

Love, Constraints, and Freedom

The knowledge that we love our teens unconditionally is one of the greatest gifts we can give them. But that does not guarantee they will follow our way. God offered unconditional love to the children of Israel, and they turned away. Hosea 11:2 depicts God's lament over Israel's ingratitude; "The more I called Israel, the further they went from me. They sacrificed to the Baals and they burned incense to images."

Listen to God's pain when He protests in Hosea 11, "It was I who taught Ephraim to walk, taking them by the arms; but they did not realize it was I who healed them" (v. 3). When our children turn away, we also look back on all we've done for them. We remember how we held them in our arms, how we literally and figuratively took them by the hand and led them. When they were sick, we nursed them back to health. We mourn when they go astray, yet we can find some solace in the fact that God, too, grieves when we turn away.

In verse 4 God explains how he guided His people. "I led them with cords of human kindness, with ties of love." God provided *constraints*—not the chains and ropes used on slaves, but the "cords of human kindness," cords that were loving, not coercive. Your children need to see the restrictions you make as cords of human kindness and ties of love, motivated by your love for them rather than your need to control them.

The second part of verse 4 goes on to describe the *freedom* God gives: "I lifted the yoke from their neck and bent down to feed them." Freedom comes when your teens no longer need external constraints because they have internalized the behavior. No child is more in bondage than the one lacking in self-discipline. Such a child is at the mercy of his or her latest impulse or craving. Personal freedom comes through self-discipline. It is your responsibility as a parent to instruct and guide your children so they can develop self-control.

Consequences Are Empowering

The consequences of turning away from God are seen in Hosea 11:5–6: "Will not they return to Egypt and will not Assyria rule over them because they refuse to repent? Swords will flash in their cities, will destroy the bars of their gates and put an end to their plans." Your children will face the natural consequences of unhappiness and difficulty in life when they turn from God's way. When this happens, don't stand back and moralize, "I told you so; you reap what you sow." Reach out with a parental covenant love to bring your wayward children in.

We must provide a way back when our children take a wrong turn. This is how God responded to His people in verses 8–10. "How can I give you up, Ephraim? . . . My heart is changed within me; all my compassion is aroused. I will not carry out my fierce anger, nor will I turn and devastate Ephraim. For I am God, and not man—the Holy One among you. I will not come in wrath." God was angry with the children of Israel. The human response would have been, "They made their bed, so let them lie in it and suffer the consequences." But God's heart changes from anger to compassion, offering a way back.

You'll be angry with your children, and you'll be tempted to let them wallow in the muddy path they've chosen. You may even want revenge because you think your kids deliberately wanted to hurt you or get back at you. When you finally get a grip on your rage, you'll have to admit that your anger is about yourself as well as your kids. You're concerned about what others will think, and it will be natural for you to take it personally when your kids make you look bad. You want them to be different—not only for their good, but for your good. It hurts when others criticize your parenting or respond to you with a raised eyebrow and a questioning glance. But anger can force you to face the fierceness of your feelings in a new way. Be willing to meet your anger head on; deal honestly with the wrath you feel so you can put it aside and let compassion take over.

A Modern Parable of Forgiveness

Eric and Sylvia Erikson have experienced these principles firsthand. Here is their personal story of restoration, told by Sylvia.

> The phone rang! It was our 18-year-old daughter, Cynthia, weeping so hard that I couldn't understand her words. I put Eric on the phone and together we tried to calm her down so she could tell us what was wrong. "Mom, Dad, I'm pregnant." We were startled but somehow found a way to keep our cool. The thousand miles separating us seemed like light years.
>
> "Honey, we're so sorry!" we told her. "We love you and wish we could be with you. Slow down and tell us what's happening. We're here to listen and to help." Cynthia went on with the disheartening facts. She had been to the doctor, the pregnancy was confirmed, she and Jerry didn't know what to do. We suggested a counselor we knew in the area and a pastor who would be a compassionate listener. Cynthia had the support of Jerry and his parents as well as some close friends.
>
> After Cynthia hung up the phone, it was our turn to react. Our emotions of shock, sadness, anger, and disbelief were tumultuous and confusing. She had always been such a good kid! We sat together in a daze, immobilized by what we'd heard. As we thought back we had to admit there had been signs! Two years

earlier, when Cynthia was still in high school, we had confronted her about being so exclusive with Jerry, who was a college senior. We had hoped she would date around a bit more and be involved in a campus ministry. The next year when Cynthia got a small apartment of her own, Jerry would frequently answer the phone when we called. It crossed our minds that they might be living together. When we asked her about it during a visit, she adamantly denied it. We backed off and tried to be supportive, even though we didn't particularly like Jerry.

These suspicions of the past haunted us, and we questioned ourselves again and again. We'd given all the guidance we knew how to give in the area of moral decision making. We'd talked openly with Cynthia about the psychological implications of engaging in sexual intercourse before marriage, as well as the risks of sexually transmitted disease and responsible use of birth control. This all seemed irrelevant now in light of the pregnancy. Cynthia had made a choice and now had to face a consequence she hadn't bargained for. Or had she? We wondered if this was her way of getting us to accept Jerry. What could we say at this point about marriage?

We felt deceived and angry. How could our beautiful, intelligent daughter get herself into this predicament? Why had she not taken seriously our discussions about the pitfalls of premarital sex? Why had she and Jerry not been more responsible about using birth control? And finally, what was this going to mean for Cynthia's future?

We needed time to do some thinking of our own. What advice could we give Cynthia at this point? Were we destined to watch her make decisions that could ruin her life? We were clearly not in control of the situation. We knew that there was no easy solution. In fact, every option she considered would have serious effects on her future. We tried to think through all the options.

What about the possibility of an abortion? That was hard to even contemplate. We worried about the psychological and spiritual ramifications; what would it mean to Cynthia as a Christian? We asked ourselves the same question, honestly discussing the pros and cons for us should they decide on this course of action.

Perhaps they would choose adoption. Since Cynthia's aunt had adopted children, we knew Cynthia would be open to this. However, we had to face the fact that if she gave the child up for adoption, we would most likely never have a chance to know our own grandchild. We were surprised at how difficult this was to accept. We had always believed adoption was the best solution to an unplanned pregnancy, but now it was *our* grandchild we were talking about.

What about marriage? We certainly didn't want to pressure Cynthia into marriage to a man we didn't think would be a good spouse for her. We could support her choice to be a single mother better than her choice to marry the wrong person. So the next question we asked ourselves was how Cynthia would support a child, raise it on her own, and how this choice would affect us. There certainly were no easy answers! We wrote a letter to let Cynthia know that we would support her in whatever choice she made.

The phone call finally came. She and Jerry loved each other, wanted to get married and raise the child that was part of their love. I was relieved they decided against abortion and adoption, but my heart sank when I heard "marriage." I wasn't prepared to accept Jerry as a son-in-law. I realized that my secret agenda was that she would choose to be a single mother.

But the choice had been made. They wrote their appreciation for our response in a carefully composed letter that revealed they had weighed all the options and they knew what they wanted. Did we feel acceptance immediately? Not really! It took time to sink in. We suggested they get married right away, but Cynthia wanted a small church wedding that would take a few months to plan. I had to let go of the fantasies I'd had about planning Cynthia's wedding day with her under much different circumstances. My heart also went out to my only daughter who had dreamed of having a beautiful wedding from the time she was a little girl. We were happy she had the emotional strength to follow through on a church wedding as a confirmation of her spiritual life.

The next week she called to say they set the date on the same day as our wedding anniversary. What did that signify? Did she hope to have a solid marriage like ours had been for over 25 years? I was touched and felt an emotional connection with her that healed much of my disappointment. I was proud of her ability to make hard decisions and take a positive attitude about this circumstance in her life.

Nine months later, we found that accepting the baby was easier than accepting our son-in-law! We had to work out the unresolved anger we had toward Jerry, and toward Cynthia too, later that year. We needed God's grace in a new way, to bring Jerry into our hearts and commit ourselves to him in a covenant love. It took some doing, but with the Lord's grace, we were able to extend the same to him.

It took a special portion of God's grace to get the Eriksons through this difficult time. We believe Sylvia and Eric acted out of unconditional love and grace, dealing appropriately with their feelings and conflicts in a godly way, so they could offer their daughter a way back. God's way is to keep the door open!

5

Growing Up in the "Just Do It" Generation

Your daughter admits, without blinking an eye, that she's had sexual intercourse with three different guys in the past two years. You've worked your way through the first four chapters of the book, but one thing still plagues you: why does she feel so *comfortable* having sex, and why is it so difficult for you to communicate to her that what she's doing is wrong?

It might help you to realize that you're not alone, and that there are some very good reasons why your daughter feels comfortable about having sex at her age. In order to understand your teenagers' sexual attitudes, you need to understand the sexually saturated world they live in.

Has there ever been a time in any society when sex has so saturated the popular culture—particularly through the mass media? We don't have to remind you how radically the commonly held views on sexuality have changed since our parents' or our own generation. Our kids are searching for values in the vast wilderness of a sexually confused society. They are barraged every day by a variety of conflicting values and beliefs about sex. It may help to give a brief historical perspective.

From Generation to Generation

Our parents and grandparents were heavily influenced by the Victorian era, a time when sexual taboos and negative messages about sex were widespread. The solution to sexual desire was simply to repress anything that appeared to be sexual. Not only was it immodest for a person's arms and legs to be uncovered in public, but even the bare legs of living room furniture needed to be covered with little skirts!

During this time in our history, a sharp line was drawn between sexual desire and love. A virtuous man was expected to wed a woman with pure thoughts. If he really loved his wife, he would abstain from having sex with her, since that would be a degrading act to a woman.

Women received similar warnings. The expert medical opinion in 1867 claimed sexual desire in a young woman to be pathological. The Surgeon General of the United States made a statement that nine-tenths of the time, "decent" women did not feel the "slightest pleasure" in sexual intercourse. And the "Ann Landers" advice columnist of 1870 wrote, "The more a woman yields to the demands of animal passion in her husband, the more he loses his love and respect for her."

The lyrics of a popular love song during the turn of the century hints at the dichotomy between sexual desire and love: "I want a girl just like the girl who married dear old Dad." We shouldn't be too surprised that a double standard flourished during this period. Men had their sexual needs met by the "bad" women, but they would only marry the "good" women. It wasn't until the "roaring 20s" that the traditional double standard was replaced by a philosophy of "permissiveness with affection." Premarital sex was okay as long as you loved your sexual partner. This was the predominant way of thinking through the 1950s.

The sexual revolution of the sixties, influenced by hippies and flower children, advocated "free love." Hugh Hefner and his *Playboy* magazine found an eager audience of adult males who were ready to jump on the "sexual freedom" bandwagon. Denying the complexities of womanhood, they proceeded to reduce women to a single dimension—a sex object. *Playboy* had great appeal to insecure males who were terrified at the thought of relating to a real, live, multidimensional woman. Unsure males were told what clothes to buy, how to wear them, what music to play on the stereo, how to mix a drink, and when to turn the lights down. In short, the message was, "how to get a woman into bed and emerge free of any emotional attachments to her." If for some unforeseen reason the young man happened to lose his heart to a woman, the Great Bunny in the sky would be quick to pronounce, "You goofed!"

Women were beginning to shake off the old ways of thinking, too. Some coeds were delighted to break the old double standard by having sex with multiple partners. Although the majority of teens and young adults still held the more conservative view and chose to have sex only with the person they intended to marry, the trend toward promiscuous or recreational sex continued to grow. Engaging in sex with multiple partners, experimenting with bisexuality, swapping marriages, and having orgies were being done in the name of free love. Clearly, society in the 1960s had become preoccupied with sex.

Our teenagers have grown up in a culture that is saturated with sex. The "anything goes if it feels good" and "just do it" generation tells teenagers that instant gratification is what counts. The television advertisement for Nike shoes shows Michael Jordan gliding through the air and—swisssh!—he executes a backwards two-handed slam dunk. The next words you hear are coordinated with the message appearing on the screen—JUST DO IT! Madison Avenue knows its audience. Appealing to the "just do it" theme, the emphasis is to act on impulse.

It doesn't take a genius to understand that the phrase "doing it" often connotes engaging in sex. Your teens are part of this "just do it" generation. They have been emersed in an adolescent popular culture which cajoles, entices, and encourages them to "do it." Teens are preoccupied with getting *it*, with little regard for any moral considerations.

Growing up fully exposed to contemporary adolescent culture is analogous to a speedboat traveling downstream through swiftly flowing rapids. The hormones, which are already vigorously cruising through the body, are propelled at raging speeds by the cultural sexual stimuli of our age.

Developmental Influences

At the same time culture is rushing our children's sexual development, their cognitive, physical, and emotional maturity is developing at a different rate. You need only to think back to your own adolescence to remember the crazy emotional ups-and-downs. For the adolescent, everything in life is a melodrama, and changes are happening constantly. Feelings are at the forefront, ranging from joy to deep despair, thrills to utter boredom, and paralyzing fear to confident action. Adolescence is a bewildering period for both you and your teens, because they are changing right before your very eyes.

You need only take a look at them to see the changes. Your son's voice is deepening, hair is growing where there was once peach fuzz, and muscles are beginning to bulge. Your daughter is developing hips, enlarged breasts, and noticeable curves. Your children's bodies were sexual from the very beginning of life; whether you noticed or not, your baby boy had occasional erections and your baby girl some vaginal lubrication. They experienced pleasurable sensations from an early age. But now the erotic aspects of sexuality emerge; the capacity of boys to ejaculate and girls to menstruate are the external signals that they can now reproduce.

At the same time, your teens are beginning to formulate a moral conscience about how to exist in their world as sexual beings. They will certainly consider your views when they begin to make decisions about sex, but the main influence will be their peers. You are losing ground to the youth culture. No longer are you in complete control of your teens' activities. Your influence is diminishing, and even though you've protected, loved, guided, and nurtured them into maturity, now they're pulling away from you to find their own way.

The Identity and Intimacy Twins

One of the stormy transitions from childhood to adulthood has to do with two important developmental tasks: establishing identity and gaining intimacy. The big question your adolescent son or daughter asks is, "Who am I?" Prior to adolescence, your children were quite content to find their identity through you. The beliefs, values, and ideals they readily took on as preadolescent children were likely a reflection of *your* ideals. They wanted to be like you. Sometimes children model their parents to such a degree that there is no sharp distinction between their values and sense of self and those of the family. In psychological terms, children have an "undifferentiated self" rooted in their parents, their family, or their community.

During adolescence, teenagers begin the differentiating process. This means they are in search of a self that is separate from parents, family, or community. Teenagers don't necessarily reject their parents' values, beliefs, and ideals, but they will certainly question them. Those beliefs and values must mean more to them than merely a reflection of their parents. This reevaluation is actually an essential aspect of identity formation, because teenagers must take on values for themselves in order to be responsible for their behaviors. If they simply adopt their parents' beliefs, or, conversely, if they simply rebel against their parents' beliefs, they have not found an identity of their own. So when your teenagers challenge your authority, they are actually right on target in their growth toward selfhood. They must find an internal authority that they can claim as their own.

Teenagers challenge their parents' beliefs for two reasons. First, they must find their own answers to questions about life. They must know _why_ they hold to certain truths. Their reasoning ability will not let them embrace values they have not defined as their own. Second, they need to make decisions about their actions that are congruent with their personal beliefs. In this way they establish their identity as individual persons. It becomes a matter of self-honor.

Along with a search for a personal identity, teenagers are dealing with the issue of intimacy. The question is, "How do I reveal myself to you?" Intimacy is the process of knowing yourself and letting others know you. It involves being vulnerable by sharing your thoughts, feelings, dreams, struggles, and the events in your life with another person. It has to do with feeling emotionally connected and in close relationship.

The quests for identity and intimacy are often so intertwined in a teenager's life that it's sometimes hard to separate the two. Can you be intimate without an identity to share? Or do you find your identity in the process of being intimate? Recent studies have pointed out that boys tend to progress faster when it comes to identity formation. The exact opposite seems to be true for teenage girls, who are more likely to develop the ability to be intimate sooner than establishing their identity. We think this difference may account for the way teenagers think about sexuality.

Your adolescent daughter may have sex to meet her desire to be intimate and close to her boyfriend. Your son, on the other hand, may have sex with his girlfriend in order to find his identity as a man. When listening to teenagers talk about why they have sex, it's not unusual for a teenage girl to say she didn't enjoy the sex that much, but she liked the feeling of being loved. Teenage boys, on the other hand, often refer to their sexual prowess. We're not suggesting that these are the only reasons teenagers engage in sex; the point is that they have other reasons than just the physical for being sexually involved.

In the interest of psychological health, we believe that sex is for adults only. Early involvement in sex can easily inhibit the personality development of adolescents. If teenagers engage in sex before they have clearly established their own identities, they risk losing themselves in the identity of their partner. They may stop asking, "Who am I?" for a while because they think they have an answer: "I am so-and-so's lover."

When your daughter has sex with a boy, it may very well be that what she wants is intimacy. In time, she will be tremendously disappointed in physical sex because it doesn't meet her real need for intimacy. In like manner, when your son has sex to establish his identity as a man, he is likely to remain unfulfilled emotionally. The psychological risk to him is that his immature intimacy skills fail to develop when he equates intimacy with sex.

This brings us back to the question at the beginning of the chapter regarding how your teenagers can be so comfortable with sex. They believe from cultural messages that sex will fulfill their psychological needs for intimacy and identity. Sex is a "quick fix," so why not "just do it?" But in reality, the only way to achieve identity and intimacy is through a process of growth and maturity.

Why Adolescence?

This is precisely the question anthropologist Margaret Mead asked when she reported on research among peoples of the South Sea Islands. In these primitive societies, Mead found no such thing as adolescent stress and strain. In fact, there was no such thing as adolescence. Coming of age in Samoa was a very different experience than coming of age in America.

Mead found only two categories of people in the societies she studied: children and adults. The children were treated like children, free from adult demands and excluded from making adult decisions. When children reached puberty, they went through well-established rites that gave them adult status. Youngsters left the village defined as children and returned as adults. It was as simple as that—as if someone put a sign around their necks announcing, "No Longer a Child!" Passage through the prescribed ritual was an infallible indication that from then onward that person was a full-fledged sexual being, awarded all the rights and responsibilities of an adult.

Alice and Alex in Wonderland

Making the transition from childhood to adulthood in our culture is much more complicated. There are no specified rites or rituals that provide a clear passage. The lack of definition for youth in American society leaves them at a loss about how to span the gulf and successfully accomplish that transition.

This ambiguity is highly stressful for adolescents in the United States. Young people are put into the precarious position of being neither man nor boy, neither woman nor girl, but somewhere in between. In our society, being a teenager is like being Alice or Alex in Wonderland trying to figure out what the rules and expectations are. Is a teenager a child or an adult? The likely response is "both" or "neither"; there is no clear definition.

Formal attempts to define adulthood in contemporary society do very little to clear up the confusion. When it comes to the question of whether a person is old enough to get married, each state determines the age of majority differently, ranging all the way from 14 for women in some states to 18 for men in others. When it comes to voting privileges or military service, a person must be 18 years of age; when it comes to driving a car, 16 is the magic number. And it's fascinating to notice how adulthood is defined when financial profit is involved. Even for pre-teens, movie theaters, airlines, buses, and most public establishments require an adult admission price. Teenagers are often required to pay adult prices, but when it comes to seeking adult privileges, they are told to wait until they grow up. No wonder it's so confusing for them! And no wonder it's so confusing for us to know how to bridge the gap!

Growing up in the United States can be compared to a jazz jam session in which musicians come together to play, but there is no written score. The musicians are free to improvise as they go along. With no clear cultural norms, adolescents improvise new ways of behaving. This explains the rapidly changing adolescent fashions and styles, whether it be clothes, hairstyles, or language.

The creation of an adolescent subculture is one way for youth in our society to establish identity. The peer group establishes the norms, such as wearing the right clothes, having the right hairstyle, playing the "in" music, speaking the "in" language, and participating in certain sexual or drug-related behaviors. The greater the insecurity of the adolescent, the more dependent he or she is on the peer group norms. And because teens today have easier access to money than previous generations, they are more independent. Parents have less influence over their teens' clothes, diets, and activities.

Disenfranchisement of Youth

Young people feel society has given them a bum rap. An analogy of driving a car might be helpful. When asked, "Who's in the driver's seat?," the typical teen perceives that the car (society) is being driven by their parents. Parents won't let their children get behind the wheel. Teens want to be in control of their lives and determine where the car is going, but parents hold on for fear they'll crash. Meanwhile, teens wonder how they're even supposed to learn if they are not given the chance to drive.

The formation of a youth culture has retarded the movement of adolescents towards adult status. Many teens experience a desolating lack of meaning in their lives.

Locked out of purposeful adulthood, sex is one behavior that seems to bring meaning in the midst of meaningless-ness. Sex becomes a pleasurable escape from the boredom of adolescent limbo.

More Than Raging Hormones

Our teenagers are bombarded with messages from our electronically oriented society enticing them to act out sexual impulses. Yet the Christian community for the most part remains silent, ignoring teenage sexuality or offering empty advice like, "Just say no to sex!"

C. S. Lewis offers a hypothetical illustration to describe a society that is saturated with sex. In his scenario, people have paid money and gathered together to view a covered platter sitting on a table. At the assigned time and to the beat of drums, someone very slowly lifts the cover of the platter and exposes the object for all to see. To the expectant eyes and everyone's surprise, on the platter is a pork chop! Lewis goes on to surmise that an observer would ask what's wrong with the eating habits of such a society. The point is well made! We must ask the same question, "What is wrong with the sexual habits of our society?"

We've actually gone a step further in the 1990's, because now the platter is no longer covered. Adolescents have been *saturated* with sex from the time they were little kids. Sex is front page news. They hear it in music, see it in the advertising media, watch it as the major theme in movies, sitcoms, and MTV music videos.

Premarital sexual standards have come a long way:

from abstinence in the 1800s, to the double standards of the early 20th century, to permissiveness with affection up until the 1960s, and finally to permissiveness without affection, an attitude which has prevailed throughout children's lifetimes. Although abstinence before marriage has always been the traditional Christian view, it's not the majority standard in our society. Even though many people, including Christians, *say* they believe premarital sex is a bad idea, when it comes to actual behavior, permissiveness with affection is the standard most people follow.

The most dangerous attitude toward sex is permissiveness without affection. In this view, sex is casual and recreational. Fewer people are willing to live by this standard since the impact of HIV. People who take the threat of AIDS seriously are not willing to die for a casual sexual encounter, no matter how much they enjoy it. This fear has bolstered a trend away from promiscuous sexual encounters and even safe sex practices and toward a return to monogamous sexual relationships. It seems a sane and healthy way to live out sexuality today. However, while this is a positive move for sexually active adults, teenagers continue to live as if nothing could ever happen to them.

We've offered some ideas in this chapter about why teenagers feel comfortable engaging in sexual intercourse. But we don't have all the answers. Your teens are unique and have different ways of putting their sexual beliefs, their standards, and their behaviors together. We hope you have gained a sympathetic understanding of the cultural and developmental influences that contribute to your children's ways of thinking and feeling about sex.

Whether or not your teenagers decide to change their sexual behavior, they need to be understood. They'll pay more attention if you show an understanding of where they're coming from. With this understanding, we believe you can help your children make better decisions about their sexual choices. The next chapter will give you some ideas about how you can guide them out of today's sexual wilderness and into a position where they can take control of their lives.

6

Why Say No to Sex?
Guiding Your Teenager Out
of the Sexual Wilderness

You may be pessimistic about your ability to influence your child's sexual behavior. You may be tempted to throw up your hands and cry, "What's the use? They're going to do what they want to do and there's nothing I can do or say that will make any difference." Some of you may be too intimidated to talk to your teens about their sexual involvement. But don't be put off! Having a sympathetic understanding of how culture has affected your teens also gives you the impetus to help them find good reasons to say NO to sex. The one thing so badly lacking in teenagers' lives today is a sound moral framework for making sexual choices. Do not give up just when your teen needs you most. This is the time when your son or daughter may be open to your ideas about the real meaning of sex.

Is Your Behavior Consistent With Your Values?

What you say to your teenagers at this point depends on what they accept as their basis for making moral decisions. Some will believe that their moral decisions should be based on biblical teaching. If this is the case, it will be fruitful to ask if their behavior is congruent with those beliefs.

You might point to appropriate scripture passages that presents sexual intercourse as a life-uniting act that seals the marital bond between husband and wife. It would be appropriate to call their attention to the *covenantal* basis for Christian marriage as modeled after the covenant God made with Abraham (Gen. 17:1–7). A covenant commitment, when compared to a contract, has to do with its unconditional nature. Covenant love is the foundation of permanence on which sexual intimacy is built. In marital relationships, trustworthiness and faithfulness give partners freedom and courage to share themselves at deeper levels. This "forever" commitment enhances the capacity to share without fear and deepens love. When partners communicate their love through thought and action, regardless of their failures and flaws, they are able to risk being "naked and not ashamed." Covenant love establishes a confidence in which there is no need to hide from one another, and partners can openly express their deep longings, concerns, failures, and needs to each other.

The biblical view is that sexual intercourse is to take place only within a *marriage* relationship. This emphasis is so strong in the Bible that two persons can be regarded to *be* married if they engage in sexual intercourse. Scripture describes the sealing of covenant commitment as becoming "one flesh" (Gen. 2:24, Matt. 19:4–6). The meaning of sexual intercourse is the uniting of two people. In 1 Corinthians 6:16–17 the apostle Paul repeats this when he writes, "For it is said, 'The two will become one flesh,' " followed by the statement, "But he who unites himself with the Lord is one with him in spirit." Paul dares to suggest that the unity which sexual intercourse is meant to establish between two people is comparable to the unity each of us is meant to experience with Jesus Christ! If your teen is a believer, he or she can not help but be sobered by the significance which the Bible assigned to sexual intercourse.

Scripture teaches that marriage between two persons results when (1) their relationship is based upon a mutually shared covenant commitment; and (2) that they consummate their union through sexual intercourse. You need to teach your teen that from a radically biblical point of view, sexual intercourse was meant to be the sealing of a marriage relationship. Emphasizing this scriptural teaching is not to deemphasize the importance of marriage, but rather to emphasize the seriousness of two persons engaging in sex.

From a biblical point of view, "premarital sex" is intercourse between unmarried persons who do not share a mutal covenant commitment. It could even be argued that there is no such thing as "premarital intercourse," only intercourse in a marriage which has not yet come into its own, or intercourse which has nothing to do with marriage. When sexual intercourse is not based upon a mutual covenant commitment, the Bible teaches it is fornication (Acts 15:20, 29; 1 Cor. 5:1, 7:2, 10:8, 6:13, 18; 2 Cor. 12:21; Gal. 5:19; Eph. 5:3, Col. 3:5; 1 Thess. 4:3).

But, does a mutual covenant determine that one is ready for intercourse? Theologically, we can only answer that God alone can judge the hearts and intentions of people. We must be open to the possibility that two people who share a covenant commitment, even though they have not gone through a legal or public marriage ceremony, are married in the sight of God when they purposely seal the covenant with sexual intercourse.

On the other hand, merely making a mutual covenant together does not automatically determine that it is expedient for the couple to seal that commitment with sexual intercourse. In 1 Corinthians 6:12 we are told, "Everything is permissible for me, but not everything is beneficial." In a social psychological sense, there is a right and wrong time to marry. The right time is when two people are mature and independent enough to be in a responsible, mutually giving relationship.

Genesis 2:24 describes this time as a leaving, uniting, and becoming "one flesh." When marriage partners have not been sufficiently differentiated from their parents, nor have they established an independent sense of self, they are not prepared to enter into a comprehensive uniting relationship. A covenant commitment requires that the couple ask what is beneficial for them, not merely what is allowed. Sexual intercourse is the seal of a mutual covenant that undergirds the uniting of two lives in a life purpose and the meaningful tasks of work, procreation, and recreation.

Is Anyone in Danger?

Perhaps your teenagers don't see any relevance between the Bible and their lives. They may feel that the Bible tells them what to do but doesn't give them a convincing reason to change their behavior. In this case, it may be more productive to have them think about the potential dangers that are part of sexual intercourse. This "morality of caution" approach can help them face the dangerous facts head on. Don't ask questions in a condemning or accusatory tone, but ask in a way that says, "Let's figure this out together." Let your teens ask their own questions as well. You'll gain insights into how they think about sex and what they worry most about.

Begin by discussing the impact their sexual activity may have on their health, their emotional well-being, and their future. "Will I get hurt—physically or emotionally—if I sleep with this person?" "What would I do if I/she got pregnant?" "What if we're sexually intimate and then break up?"

Encourage your teens to think about their sexual partner as well as themselves. "What if my girlfriend has to have an abortion?" "What if my boyfriend and I have to get married? Do we love each other enough?" "Who else have I (or my partner) slept with? What if I am (or he/she is) HIV positive?"

Help your child realistically examine his or her own maturity and that of the sexual partner. "Do I feel good about having sex with this person?" "Do I get upset when he doesn't call me or looks at another girl?" "Do I brag about our sexual activity to my friends?" "How is my sexual behavior affecting my relationship with my family, my friends, and God?"

Will It Enrich the Relationship?

"But, Mom and Dad, we love each other so much! We couldn't possibly hurt each other!" Many teens are well beyond the "puppy love" stage. The feelings they have for their boyfriend or girlfriend are very real. As a parent, you should take their love and commitment seriously. But you should also ask them questions about how sex may effect their relationship, both now and in the future. Will sex enhance or destroy their commitment? Will it help them grow together or grow apart? The point of these questions is to keep the relationship in focus and help your teenager and his or her partner assume mutual responsibility for it.

Help the two of them discuss their sexual relationship together. The most important questions they must ask themselves are, "Is this the right time for us to be sexual? Am I committed enough to my partner to get married should there be a pregnancy? Can we trust each other to be faithful in a covenant, forever loving? Can we allow each other personal freedom while working together to build a strong union?"

Setting up a nonjudgmental atmosphere will help them answer these questions honestly. It's risky for both you and your teens, because there are no guarantees on the answers. The young couple may confirm that they are doing the best thing for themselves, each other and the relationship. On the other hand, they may reconsider their decision after discovering the inconsistencies in their thinking. The main goal here is to get them to think about the realities of the relationship and acknowledge the pros and cons—and the sooner, the better.

The following example of Chad and his girlfriend Elise shows what can happen if teenage couples don't think honestly and realistically about the implications of their sexual intimacy.

Chad and Elise decided to move in together because they believed it would enhance their relationship. However, it didn't occur to them how difficult it would be for their families when people at church started asking questions. So Chad and Elise stopped going to church. When they began having difficulty with finances, they blamed each other for not contributing equally to the household. Soon they were at each other's throats. Neither family was willing to bail them out. A decision they thought would enhance their relationship actually ended up destroying it. They eventually split up because they found there wasn't enough mature love to keep the relationship going. It was a painful separation, and they each suffered emotionally. They thought sexual intimacy could sustain their relationship, but now all they were left with were the scars of failure.

Evaluating Reasons for Engaging in Sex

Contrary to what many people may think, God's rules about sexual behavior aren't meant to deprive us of sexual pleasure. But they do insure that we are ready for the pleasure of a loving, trusting, and deeply satisfying relationship. Many people believe that *all* sex outside of marriage is wrong—no ifs, ands, or buts. We aren't convinced, however, that it's quite that simple.

We believe that God wills for all sexual intercourse to take place within marriage. But having said this, we hasten to add that not all types of sexual relationships outside of marriage are equal in the way they transgress God's desire. Some teens choose to engage in premarital sex, but only with the person they intend to marry. Others are sexually promiscuous, having impersonal, indiscriminate sex with a number of different partners. Your teenager may be having sex for the right reason at the wrong time, or for the wrong reason at the wrong time.

Ron and Sylvia Cashion are the parents of 22-year-old Shannon and 16-year-old Kimberly. They recently discovered that both of their daughters were having sex. Shannon has been in an exclusive relationship with her boyfriend Dave for four years. During the last three months she and Dave have been sexually intimate. They justify this to themselves because they have pledged an exclusive love for each other. Kimberly, on the other hand, has slept with eight different boys, some on the first date and some during relationships that lasted over several weeks.

The Cashions are right to be concerned about the sexual involvement of both daughters. They should not feel pressured into agreeing with Shannon and Dave's position that "commitment to love" is all that is needed to legitimize sexual involvement. But they should be far more concerned with the sexual behavior of Kimberly. Her promiscuity is symptomatic of a deeper problem. They must ask probing questions about what motivates her to engage in sex with so many partners in non-committed relationships. And they must convince her to confront her own life-threatening behavior.

Sex for the Right Reason at the Wrong Time

Let's look first at the situation of Dave and Shannon. They each worked hard to make it through college and establish their independence, yet they still find themselves financially dependent on their parents. They've achieved the emotional maturity to make a marriage commitment, but they can't "live on love alone" at this point in their lives.

As parents, we should begin by sympathizing with them in their dilemma. It's not as easy as it used to be for newlyweds to attain financial stability. But we should point out to Dave and Shannon that if they choose to be sexually intimate, they settle for one small part of a committed relationship and shortchange themselves of the total package. Sexual intercourse may only confound their relationship; until they manage their life together financially and enter into the adventure of setting up a household, they are living out only half their dream. Bonding in marriage requires intimacy and vulnerability in all aspects of life together. Sex may help Dave and Shannon feel close emotionally, but it could cripple them individually. The relationship may simply limp along without the benefit of total togetherness.

Dave and Shannon need to understand intimacy as something that develops in day-to-day living—through joy, pain, frustration, vulnerability, and accountability in all aspects of life. Since they are only bonding sexually, they are likely to hold back, afraid to risk disclosing other parts of their lives.

Marriage would test Dave and Shannon to the breaking point but also lead them to new levels of growth that they cannot begin to understand in their present arrangement. Only a full-time marital arrangement gives sufficient security to work through all the fears and joys that bring a couple to higher levels of intimacy.

Sex for the Wrong Reasons at the Wrong Time

If, like Kimberly, your teenager is having sex for the wrong reasons, it's harder to have sympathy for her behavior. Who wants to face the fact that their daughter's emotional problems are leading her to act out in sexual ways? You know she is at risk and needs help. It's easy to point out why she shouldn't engage in sex, but she's going to need more help than that. What are the emotional needs that drive teenagers like Kimberly to engage in frequent, casual, and even dangerous sex?

Using Sex as a Substitute for Emotional Intimacy

Many sexually promiscuous teens have a deep longing for emotional love. But their low self-esteem leads them to believe they are unlovable, so they give their bodies as a substitute. They may experience physical pleasure, but it never delivers the emotional intimacy they desire. Sadly, these young people may go from one sexual relationship to another, only perpetuating the belief that there is nothing about them that attracts others. Their self-esteem declines even more as they feel like a sex object.

Other promiscuous teenagers actually have a great fear of emotional intimacy. They haven't yet learned how to be emotionally intimate, and they deceive themselves into thinking that physical intimacy equals emotional intimacy. They hide behind this illusion, and if a partner wants more from them emotionally, they run because they know they can't deliver what they don't have. They're likely to dump that person and look for another sexual encounter.

Having Sex Because You Can't Say No

Many teenagers are not strong enough to say no, especially to someone they admire or fear. So they give in to physical sex while remaining emotionally detached. They don't want to have sex and they don't enjoy it. But fear of rejection, ridicule, or even emotional or physical attack overrides their sensibilities.

While working for the housing department at a large university, I met a college freshman named Dane whose inability to say no to peers led to tragedy. Dorm mates had learned that Dane was a virgin and began harassing him about it. They set him up with a girl for the purpose of "helping him become a real man." There was a big party on the fourth floor that night to celebrate his lost virginity. The dorm mates felt triumphant, but Dane was crushed by his failure to resist their pressure. He was so distraught about going against his personal and religious standards, he attempted suicide the next day.

When a teenager's ego strength or identity is underdeveloped, the testing of his sexual values can be a tremendous challenge for him. Dane was vulnerable and found it especially tough to assert his values in a non-Christian environment. Having sex with the girl had to do with proving something to his friends rather than expressing authentic affection to a person he loved. You need to help your teenagers believe that they *always* have the right to say no. Help to build their self-esteem and self-respect so they won't find themselves at the mercy of others.

Worshipping the Sex God

When sex becomes a god that supposedly satisfies all needs, teens are disillusioned into expecting too much from sex. They end up having sex when they're bored, when they hurt, when they're lonely, when they're anxious—whenever they want to escape life's problems. Expecting too much from sex leaves teens constantly dissatisfied; they're looking to sex as a fix rather than an experience of authentic love with another person. But they keep trying, hoping for a satisfaction they'll never achieve.

Using Sex to Get a Relationship Started or Keep It Going

Here sex becomes a weapon to control or trick the partner into staying in a relationship. The following story illustrates how this tactic can sabotage a relationship.

Kristin remembers going to the Junior-Senior prom with Chuck and being so "in love" with him that night. They came home at midnight and slow-danced to records in her living room. Kristin felt "butterflies" in her stomach and thought for sure this was a sign of true love. One thing lead to another, and soon they were petting heavily, just short of intercourse. The next few weeks Chuck and Kristin spent every waking moment together. Chuck began pushing for more physical involvement, even though Kristin wanted to back up a step or two.

That's when Chuck started giving her guilt trips about what she owed him. After all, "they'd been physically involved and she was obligated to marry him," he said. His constant pressure made Kristin feel trapped. Fraught with anxiety and fear, she turned to her parents. They listened quietly as she confessed the embarrassing details of their sexual involvement. They helped her think through the muddy situation with supporting comments. "If he really loved you, Kristin, he wouldn't try to control or badger you into doing things you don't want. He'd be glad that you want to go on to college and continue your education. He wouldn't pressure you into marriage." Kristin instinctively knew they were right. She decided to spend less time with Chuck and more time with her other friends.

As she began to pull away, Chuck became desperate. He made ugly scenes in front of her friends and threatened suicide. He was more unstable than Kristin had imagined, and now she felt more guilty than ever, believing it was her duty to save him from his despair. Her parents and friends helped her gain a different perspective. Chuck was manipulating her out of his needs, not out of love for her.

Finally she had the courage to break it off. Chuck called her parents, saying Kristin should marry him because they'd had sex. Her parents stood behind their daughter, affirming that although sexual involvement had been a mistake, it didn't obligate Kristin to marry him. Kristin learned the important difference between sexual feelings and committed love. She was grateful to her parents who were able to help her grow through this difficult situation.

Sex as a Vehicle for Pathological Needs

Rape, incest, and sexual abuse are examples of hostile, invasive sex. Perpetrators have one purpose in mind: to satisfy their own needs without regard for the victim. Because they are filled with self-hate, offenders use sex to reassure themselves of their adequacy. Pathological sexual desire can afflict teenagers as well as adults. A teenage boy who feels emotionally inadequate might coerce his date into having sex against her will. If you suspect your teen of being involved in violating sex, seek professional help immediately.

Sex as an Addiction

People can be addicted to a variety of sexual behaviors: voyeurism, exposing genitals, viewing pornography, masturbating, or sex with prostitutes. These types of compulsive sexual activity are substitutes for restlessness and loneliness. Sexual addicts often feel shame and regret after engaging in the behavior because it goes against their personal value system. Yet they are caught in a cycle they can't break. They usually make efforts to control their behavior, but anxiety builds up until they eventually give in and get the sexual "fix." Acting out the sexual behavior brings a temporary release, then the cycle begins again, becoming more intense and frequent.

Teenagers are not immune to sexual addictions, and you may wish to be informed about this problem. Patrick Carnes' book, *A Gentle Path through the Twelve Steps,* is a comprehensive guidebook to helping people with sexual addictions.

Sex for Pleasure

Sex without love is simply a physical event involving two bodies. A teenager who has sex for pleasure only wants the sensation, not the person who brings it. Focusing on physical pleasure keeps teenagers from going deeper into themselves or their partner. Immature teenagers may not have a clue about giving themselves emotionally to another person. They only know how to take what feels good, like a small child. Remaining fixated on externals, pleasure-seeking teens never find an internal self. They fool themselves into thinking that sex satisfies their deepest longings. To cover their disappointment when it doesn't, they try to get even more. They have little to give, but they know how to take.

Let's Surprise Our Teens With Answers

The mass media continually bombard our teenagers with messages that sanction sexual activity before mar-

riage. At the very height of their strongest biological
sexual urges, they are besieged by constant sexual stimulation. Even when they've committed themselves to abstinence before marriage, they face a tremendous struggle to
say no to sex.

We're beginning to see some backlash to our society's
sexual overexposure. A trend toward a new virginity
emerged in the 1980s when young coeds began to question
why they had succumbed to a standard that reduced sex to
a sensation instead of a relationship. Prior to the sexual
revolution of the 1960s, women had always been intent on
keeping emotional intimacy an essential part of a sexual
relationship. Many young people now see the shallowness
in experiencing sex as merely a pleasurable act. We should
be encouraged to see young people assert their decision to
remain celibate or monogamous and declare a rousing
"NO" to sex before marriage.

You as a parent need to be ready for your teens' sexual
bewilderment and their desperate need for guidance
through this jungle of sexual alternatives. And you also
need to be ready when they make mistakes and unwise
choices. Prepare yourself with these questions: Can you
surprise your teens with a compassionate affirmation of the
erotic in them? Can you surprise them by communicating
values that will empower them to express their sexuality
appropriately—in ways that are in harmony with their
Christian beliefs? Can you surprise them by offering
knowledge about sex and a relevant value system that
builds their self-esteem?

7

Reclaiming Virginity

Even though we can never erase the past, teenagers who have had intercourse can reclaim their virginity and commit themselves to celibacy once again. You can help your teens by adopting the attitude modeled by Jesus in his encounter with the woman caught in adultery (John 8:4). The outraged crowd said that she should be stoned, but Jesus did not condemn; he told her to go and sin no more.

Showing compassion does not mean compromising standards. We continually uphold the standards we think are right, articulating the important reasons behind them. Sexually active teens who want to recommit themselves to celibacy need parental support. We must continue to acknowledge their sexuality as they strive to make changes in their behavior and become sexually responsible. This chapter offers some strategies for helping teens reestablish a sexual value system they can live by.

Going the Second Mile

Your teenagers are in charge of their own sexual lives, and you can't always be there to monitor their behavior. As a parent, you're limited in what you can do to keep your child sexually safe. But you *can* go the second mile when sexual mistakes have been made. If you keep the communication lines open and continue to talk about sex in a frank, relaxed manner, you can be a resource for them as they make future decisions. Be ready to express well-constructed sexual values without blaming and shaming. Help your children build their own value system that informs and directs them in their future choices.

Can you admit to your teens that you don't have all the answers and that you grapple with sexual values even as an adult? Perhaps sharing a mistake you made as a teenager will help your kids see your humanness. That's what Lucy Caldwell did after her daughter Trish came to talk to her about "going too far" on a date.

Lucy wanted her daughter to see the importance of being strong enough to say no to sex. She told Trish about her own frustration as a shy, unassertive young girl at fourteen. Lucy was pretty, and many boys were attracted to her. She was both flattered and scared, since she didn't know how to act around boys. Dan liked her inexperience and naivete, and he started hanging around. He walked her to class, came to her house after school, and went to the junior high dances with her.

One afternoon they went to a movie and sat in the last row of the balcony. The movie was a more explicit one than Lucy had ever seen before, and it aroused sexual feelings in both of them. Dan began touching her in subtle but erotic ways in the dark. Lucy didn't know how to tell him to stop. She tried to push Dan's hands away but he persisted. Much to Lucy's chagrin, she was overwhelmed by her inability to be firm.

The next day she avoided Dan, figuring the only way she could stop his advances was to stop the friendship. A few weeks later, she got an anonymous phone call that devastated her. The boy on the other end of the phone asked her "how it felt to be felt by Dan." Lucy was speechless and humiliated when he laughed and hung up. It hurt to know that Dan was telling stories about her to his friends.

Lucy revealed to Trish the shame she had felt, and she also told her how the incident had helped her to change. She realized she needed more confidence in herself so she could say no when she meant no. She decided to spend time around boys in a group situation instead of putting herself in the precarious position of single dating. Her self-concept grew as she interacted with a gang of friends who had good, clean fun together. No one was exclusively romantic, and there was a wonderful freedom in their play, laughter, group hugs, talks and just being together. This is where she learned how to be comfortable with boys. In this group she began asserting her opinions and was respected for her views. It was a turning point in her life.

Trish appreciated the fact that her mother could share something so personal and painful from her teenage years. It helped her see a side of her mother she hadn't known before. She didn't feel quite so bad about the sexual mistakes she had confessed to her mother the week before. She was encouraged by the thought that she could make a new start even after her mistakes.

Be Realistic About the Gray Areas

Offering your teens a list of sexual "don'ts" isn't enough to help them resist the pressures to have sex. In order to acknowledge and celebrate their sexual feelings and desires, you must give them guidelines about what they *can* do to express themselves as sexual persons.

Your affirmation of your teens' sexuality should be as strong as your attempts to restrain their sexual impulses. Don't leave sexual expression to their imagination. Talk about the kinds of touch that express affection, the comfort of holding and being held, the joys of kissing. They'll be intrigued when you give them some positive ideas about dating rather than just a list of what not to do. Throughout the discussion, emphasize the relational aspect of intimacy; remind them to share thoughts, ideas, and feelings as well as touches.

Celibacy does not equal sexual *in*activity, as we've already said in an earlier chapter. We need to help teens make wholesome decisions about the many ways they can express themselves as sexually integrated persons. Responding to erotic stimulation in positive, pleasurable ways won't necessarily conflict with their moral belief system. But sexual expression requires self-awareness, knowledge, and discipline. Your teens need to think seriously about those gray areas: petting, masturbation, eroticism and sexual fantasies. Here are some discussion suggestions you can use to get them thinking.

Petting: A Way to Express Affection

Christians in the New Testament were told, "Greet one another with a holy kiss." The holy kiss is not clearly defined, but this verse alludes to the fact that people can express appropriate affection for each other with physical contact.

Petting or "making out" are terms that describe physical affection between people who are romantically involved. Petting behaviors range from holding hands to genital contact just short of sexual intercourse. All unmarried people, not just teenagers, must come to grips with the fuzzy areas of appropriate sexual touch in their close relationships.

Most of us would agree that touch is a wonderful way to let people know they are loved. Teenagers show their affection to their friends by putting an arm around a shoulder or giving a big bear hug at the end of a football game. When teens feel romantic with each other, it's natural for them to show affection through touch. Setting up hard and fast rules about how, when and where to touch is difficult, to say the least. Teens and their parents must consider each relationship unique. The ages and maturity of the two teens, the level of commitment, the length of the courtship and/or engagement, closeness to the marriage ceremony, and many other factors will affect the decisions you make.

Love shown through touch meets a basic human

need. Alleviate your teens' fears that you're going to recommend a "no touch" policy. Instead ask questions like, "At what point does physical touching become sexually arousing?" and "What kind of touch is appropriate at what stage in your dating relationship?" The following principles may help answer these questions.

1. *Does the degree of sexual intimacy correspond to the degree of love and commitment present in the relationship?* Physical intimacy was meant to enhance the expression of love, not dominate it. Committed lovers enjoy touching each other in many different ways that affirm their love, but they want the type, quality, and quantity of touch to correspond to the level of commitment. Your teens may decide to limit physical affection so that all facets of their relationship can grow together at similar rates.

2. *The law of diminishing returns,* a principle from physics, helps us understand that the strength of a response to a stimulus can diminish over time. In order to get the same response, we have to experience the stimulus more and more. Remember your very first kiss? A first kiss always has a special zing. But as a relationship grows, one simple kiss doesn't have quite the same zing anymore. Stronger sexual stimuli are needed to get that zing.

Sexual touch arouses our bodies, souls and minds toward the ultimate goal of physical and emotional orgasm. Our bodies are designed to respond to erotic feelings so there is increasing heartbeat, blood flow, muscular tension. Once the body is in gear, the natural inclination is to go toward the physical release. The physical and psychological buildup leaves both partners frustrated when the intended culmination is not achieved.

The closer a couple gets to the point of orgasm, the harder it becomes to return to a reduced state of arousal. For the sake of the relationship, then, your teens need to make early decisions about how much stimulation will occur. They must be clear about what triggers the physical buildup and where they must stop to cool down. A mutual decision made ahead of time alleviates the situation when bodies demand more.

I've been reminiscing about our courtship while writing this book at my in-laws' home in central California. Thirty-five years ago Jack and I courted in this very place during pre-engagement years. We had made a commitment, but we waited three years to complete our education before we married. This family home was a place where we learned about each other emotionally, spiritually, and sexually. We spent time together with Jack's family during the summers, since we were apart during the school year.

On the couch in the family room we expressed our physical affection for each other. It was a safe, semi-private place to enjoy giving and receiving love. We had made a mutual decision not to have intercourse prior to our wedding night, but this didn't mean we had a "hands off" policy. In this home, we were comfortable with the level of physical expression we had set for ourselves. Jack's home was a good place for us to keep alert to the boundaries we had agreed on. We didn't have to find a place outside the home, since Jack's parents supported our affectionate relationship. They affirmed our love, trusted our commitment, and gave us permission to have some privacy in their home for that natural expression.

Courtship was a time of discovery about many aspects of our lives. Our sexual passion was an important part of that discovery, and we found that the boundaries we set up were not incompatible with the freedom we had in expressing our love. We kept our vows to each other, and our honeymoon became a time to learn how to mesh together in sexual unity. We believe our decision contributed to the vital sexual relationship in our marriage today.

3. *Each partner must test his or her personal motive for the physical involvement and activity.* Help your teens assess their motives for physical involvement. Is their behavior an expression of affection or a desire to sexually excite the other and oneself? It's natural for both boys and girls to feel a sense of power and control when they know that they can sexually excite their partner. But this desire to build up their egos has little to do with love.

4. *Two people involved in a romantic relationship need to continually communicate about all areas of the relationship.* Help your teenager recognize the "red flags" when the physical dimension of the relationship grows out of proportion to the social, emotional, psychological, and spiritual dimensions of the relationship. Lopsidedness is not a healthy condition. Fullness in a relationship comes through honest communication where both partners disclose and share many aspects of their lives together. You may want to share some valuable insights from your own marriage about the time you spend listening, understanding, appreciating, and showing compassion for your spouse.

Emphasize to your teenagers that the "falling in love" stage won't last forever. Don't deprecate their wonderful feelings of being in love, but stress that it's a unique experience and can be somewhat fanciful. It's a time when two people are totally caught up with each other as they share thoughts, feelings, dreams, and their very selves. It can be a narcissistic experience—a bit like falling in love with yourself, because your partner reflects yourself back to you by listening and responding to you intently. You are at the center of each other's world. But falling in love is just one stage of a relationship; the nitty gritty is yet to come.

Share romantic memories of your "in love" days. Let your children know how you cherished this special time, but also help them see the beauty of a relationship that deepens through laughter and tears, dreams and struggles, togetherness and separateness. The spiritual oneness that comes through a history of interdependence is one you wouldn't trade for the world.

5. *Both partners need to take responsibility for establishing guidelines and setting physical limits in the relationship.* Help your sons reject the societal norm that says boys can go as far as they want sexually, since it's up to the girl to set the limits. Both partners together are responsible for their level of sexual involvement. One partner may want to break a boundary at some time, but since the decision was mutually agreed upon, the boundary stands. This eliminates the problem of one person giving in to the other in the heat of passion, regretting it, and then blaming the partner later. There are times when the couple may want to rethink an established boundary or may want to set a more stringent limit. They should do this at a time when they can rationally look at the pros and cons of the proposed change.

6. *Let the decision be guided by the partner with the strongest felt limits.* Most teenagers in relationships will have differing views on what the limits should be. In a committed relationship, neither partner will try to intimidate the other by judging the other's standards as prudish. Teach your teenager that intimidation destroys rather than enhances love. A loving partner will uphold the limit, rather than dismiss it and push the friend to go further. Both teens need to accept and recognize differences without criticizing or judging.

Masturbation: A Way to Remain Celibate

When we ask our teenagers to remain celibate, what do we offer as an alternative? Perhaps it's time to rethink what we say about masturbation. Could it be that this is God's way of helping teenagers recognize the sexual and raging hormones within, while giving them a means of remaining faithful to scripture concerning premarital sex? Let's take some time to discuss this controversial topic.

A boy typically engages in self-stimulation at an early age, most likely because he has easy access to his genitals. Unfortunately, a girl's first discovery of pleasurable genital sensations often comes when a boy stimulates her. Girls are given the message very early in life not to touch themselves below the waist. We think it's unfortunate that a young girl discovers the pleasures of her body by being sexually involved with a boy, rather than learning about and affirming her sexual feelings through self-discovery. Masturbation is almost a universal experience, and studies suggest that nearly all males (96%) and most females

(68%) have stimulated themselves to orgasm at some time in their lives.

In recent history, a number of myths were fabricated to discourage children from masturbating. Folk wisdom claimed such punishments as hair falling out, breaking out with warts or pimples, going blind, and becoming impotent. What should our view of masturbation be and what should we teach our children? Obviously, we can begin by dismissing the above-mentioned myths that may have perpetuated fears and guilt. We believe it's natural for children to explore their bodies and become aware of their anatomy. It's a way of affirming the sexual parts that make them human beings.

The Bible is virtually silent when it comes to the topic of masturbation. Any case a person builds, either for or against masturbation, is based on inference made from biblical passages. We find three major differences of opinion about the place of self-stimulation in a Christian's life. The most _restrictive_ position is that masturbation, under any circumstance, is sinful. The most _permissive_ position holds that masturbation under any circumstance is healthy and morally permissible. A more _moderate_ view holds that masturbation can be healthy and morally appropriate, but also has the potential to be unhealthy and immoral.

We hold to this third position as the most reasonable one. Masturbation can be a healthy way for persons to be in touch with the sexual side of themselves and to learn about sexual gratification without a partner. We believe God has given us this provision as an affirmation of our sexuality and to help us remain sexually responsible.

Self-stimulation offers an opportunity for teenagers to learn about their bodies and experience the sexual enjoyment it brings. Being in touch with yourself and your pleasurable sensations is a self-enhancing experience. Teenagers need to be relieved of the guilt surrounding masturbation and see it as one way to affirm their sexuality. If a teen doesn't masturbate, this is a personal choice that must be affirmed; it is in no way a sign of deficiency. For all young people, self-stimulation is a sexual *option*, not a requirement.

We urge you talk to your teenagers on an on-going basis about their sexual development, hormones, menstruation, wet dreams, sexual tensions, and self-stimulation. The following conversation between John and his son, Brad, may give you some ideas for discussions.

Brad had just started dating a young girl, and John was well aware of his son's enlivened sexual appetite. He wisely took the opportunity to talk with Brad about his sexual feelings and discussed with him how masturbation might be a way to keep him from acting out his impulses with his new girlfriend. It was a relief to Brad, who had not known how to handle his erotic feelings.

John went on to explain how he had used masturbation as a way to deal with his own sexual tensions when he was stationed overseas in the Navy. He thought of his girlfriend during the self-stimulation, and he felt it was a good way to keep himself connected with her and true to her. John cautioned his son about the use of pornographic materials during masturbation because they degrade women. John felt this is what the scriptures referred to as lust. He suggested that Brad might want to imagine his future wife as a way of keeping himself pure for her, rather than fantasize about an anonymous centerfold model.

You may not choose exactly this approach with your teenagers. The important point is that you're willing to talk openly with them about masturbation. It helps them know masturbation doesn't have to be a deep, dark secret. You may even want to discuss with them your mixed feelings about whether it's a good or bad thing.

One mother came to us with concern about her daughter, who had no friends and was hiding herself away in her room, reading racy romance novels. For this girl, self-stimulation caused guilt feelings and contributed even further to her negative self-image. Her mother saw her behavior as destructive; it kept her secluded and helped her escape rather than face life as a sexual person. This mother needed to address her concerns to her daughter in an honest way, without condemnation and with compassion and understanding.

When you talk openly with your teenagers about masturbation, they'll be able to share their ideas and feelings. It may help them to talk about stressful times in their lives when they feel more need for masturbation, such as during final exams. They can begin to see self-stimulation as a way to reduce anxiety.

Of utmost importance is helping your teens determine when masturbation helps them and when it hinders. Masturbation can lead to problems in marital sexuality when it's done with guilt. Teens may develop patterns of hurrying through the stimulation without really enjoying it. They may become unable to talk about sex at all because of its constant association with guilt. Compulsive masturbation, like any other compulsive behavior, is always harmful. Obsessive self-stimulation quickly becomes an addictive, shameful, self-defeating practice. In this case, teens need help from a professional.

We suggest that you spend time thinking through your own position on masturbation before talking with your teenagers. Try to understand where your reactions and ideas come from, so you are clear about why you believe the way you do. Then talk with your teens about your ideas and even your confusion. Don't forget to let them express their ideas. Try to present self-stimulation as a normal, human desire, even if you think your teenager should try to avoid it.

Fantasy: A Way to Remain Faithful

You can't talk to your teens about masturbation without talking to them about fantasy. These two topics go hand in hand, because most people fantasize when they masturbate. We need to help teenagers grasp the distinction between fantasy and lust. Jesus addresses this in Matthew 5:27-28 when he says, "You have heard that it was said, 'Do not commit adultery.' But I tell you that anyone who looks at a woman lustfully has already committed adultery with her in his heart." Lust can be defined as "extreme desire" that leads to the actual acting out of that desire. When you actually take a person into your heart and mind, you will likely pursue that person in order to have them in real life as well. The Ten Commandments speak against both coveting another person's spouse and committing adultery.

Fantasy gets a bad rap. We don't think that fantasizing about someone is necessarily the same as lusting after them, as many suggest. In fact, fantasy is a God-given ability to imagine the future in ways that propel us toward our goals. Thinking about the future gives us the incentive to work toward our goals: marrying the one we love, having children, building a successful career, and living a life according to the laws of God. Fantasy can help us visualize the goals we want to achieve.

Unfortunately, fantasy can also be an unrealistic escape that hinders growth. Jennifer was home for summer vacation after a frustrating freshman year at college. She was lonely, had never dated, and rarely participated in activities with friends. She had suffered depression off and on all year, wondering why no one was attracted to her. She dreaded going back to school in the fall. One day while she was sun bathing in the back yard, the next-door neighbor started talking to her. He was friendly and playful, and suddenly Jennifer felt very attractive. He mentioned what a nice tan she had and how she must have lots of dates in school. This was just what Jennifer needed to heal her wounded ego. Soon she found herself going out in the backyard each day in hopes of talking to Tom Davis.

Tom made a special effort to chat with Jennifer whenever he saw her. Even though he was a married man, she began to fantasize about him. She imagined his advances becoming physical and found herself feeling quite sexually stimulated by the thought. She took that thought into her bedroom and began dreaming about her romantic and sexual feelings. Occasionally she masturbated with him in mind.

Even though Jennifer would never think of breaking up a marriage, she loved daydreaming about Tom. She wasn't so depressed when she escaped into her dream world. It helped her forget about her fears of having to go back to college and interact with friends her own age. She stopped going to the church youth group and spent the summer reading novels and living with her fantasy.

But one day her fantasy became a reality. Tom knocked on her back door while she was home alone and she invited him in. He grabbed her in his arms and kissed her hard on the mouth. "I find you very attractive. Let's find a more comfortable place where we can get better acquainted," he suggested. She was frightened now. Even though part of her had wanted this to happen for the last two months, another part of her was appalled by what was happening. Her innocent flirtation and fantasies had become full-blown reality. Finally Jennifer pushed Tom away and asked him to leave. He was confused and left in a huff. Jennifer crumpled to the kitchen floor, shaking with tears, frightened about what could have happened. How did she let herself get into this situation, and who could she possibly talk to about what happened? She needed help but didn't know where to turn.

Taking an innocent fantasy and turning it into deep desire for a real person is lust. Such fantasies evoke guilt and shame, leaving a person miserable and lonely. Jennifer dehumanized Tom by converting him into a private fantasy to help her feel good about herself. Believing the fantasy could never really happen made Jennifer feel less guilty. But she was merely lying to herself.

Both single and married people sometimes fantasize in

order to increase sexual desire. When watching a movie or reading a novel, it's natural to imagine yourself in the action. There is a difference, however, between being allowing a book or movie to stir up sexual desire and lusting for a person you want to have actual sex with. Lust has to do with wanting something badly and taking steps to fulfill that desire. Fantasy, on the other hand, occurs when one wishes for something in a general sense, without an attempt to achieve that exact desire. We believe teens need to make a purposeful choice about their fantasy life, deciding whether the fantasies are in line with their personal moral value system. They can then decide which fantasies to let in and which to keep out.

Some teenagers rightfully fantasize about a future marriage partner. If that fantasy turns into lust for a specific person, it should be an important warning signal. But dreaming about a future spouse gives teens the desire to plan for the event. They may fantasize about a future mate as a way to keep from being involved sexually with dating partners. In this case, fantasy becomes a way for them to keep themselves for the one they believe God intends them to marry. Not long ago, we were at the wedding of a friend's son and noticed the special bond and love between the groom and his groomsmen. Living together for four years in the dorm at a Christian university, they had become extremely close buddies. They had made a vow to each other to uphold celibacy as a God-given blessing.

This was the first wedding of the bunch. Eric was getting married to his college sweetheart. The rehearsal dinner was a festive celebration, as all their friends toasted their love for this young couple. The entire wedding party gathered around them to pray God's blessing on their life. Then, on the wedding day, Eric's friends gave him the high-five sign after they were pronounced husband and wife. "Do us proud!" was their cheer, and the entire wedding party smiled, for they knew the meaning of that message. It said, "Take this woman and gently love her with all the passion you have. Enjoy the union of flesh you've patiently waited for, and be richly blessed." This was more than a fantasy—it was real life!

Pornography

We can't talk about masturbation and fantasy without dealing with pornography. Self-stimulation and fantasy are often connected with pornographic materials. Pornography depicts harmful and distorted attitudes toward women, children, and even sometimes toward men. According to recent studies, pornography leads to weakened moral standards. When dealing with erotic material, we must ask the questions, "Is this material dehumanizing? Does it make the people involved objects instead of real human beings?" God views humans as his cherished and valued creation. We must do no less.

Mark came to his dad with this sad story which illustrates how pornography can take a toll on someone's life. During Thanksgiving vacation, Mark had a heart-to-heart talk with his dad about something that was bothering him. Mark had been happily married for two years, and he let his Dad know how thankful he was for the Christian upbringing his parents had given him. But he'd made a choice in high school that was affecting his marriage. He didn't know where to turn for help. "I never knew that watching X-rated videos one night with some friends would affect me now," Mark confessed. "We thought we were such hot shots. I guess we were just rebelling. Some of what we saw was really sickening, but none of us would admit it. But here I am after being married for two years, and it's still hard to keep those scenes out of my mind. I hate it because I know it harms my relationship with Tami. I think about that rotten stuff instead of my beautiful wife."

Mark hung his head as he confessed and sought his father's advice. They talked together about the temptation men have to view pornographic material. David was compassionate and caring as he responded to Mark. He, too, had dealt with similar temptations in his past and could empathize. The confession was the beginning of change. They decided that when scenes came into Mark's mind, he would lay these scenes symbolically on the altar and give them over to God. Mark might not be able to keep the thoughts from entering his head, his father said, but he could decide how long they stayed there and what to do with them. They both knew that fantasies can keep you emotionally removed from the person you love. Knowing he could make a choice about it gave Mark hope. They ended their time together with prayer. Mark left home that weekend with a renewed vision of how to love his wife with his whole heart.

How can you help your teenagers select fantasies that are in keeping with God's intended desire? Encourage them to ask themselves these questions: "Is there anything de-humanizing about our fantasy? Is it directed toward a real person I'd like to have sex with? How is this fantasy affecting my life and the lives of the people I love? Is this fantasy helping me plan my future life? Or is it keeping me from developing real, healthy relationships?"

Your teens will have attained new maturity when they can make conscious choices about what they allow into their minds, hearts, and souls. When a fantasy is not in keeping with God's design for sexual integrity, they must denounce it and keep it out of their imagination. Encourage your teens to draw on God's help and discernment.

Freedom in Christ

The apostle Paul had some good things to say about balancing the need for rules and restraints with the message that we are free in Christ.

> "Everything is permissible for me"—but not everything is beneficial. "Everything is permissible for me"—but I will not be mastered by anything. "Food for the stomach and the stomach for food"—but God will destroy them both. The body is not meant for sexual immorality, but for the Lord, and the Lord for the body. (1 Cor. 6:12–13)

When it comes to expressing sexuality, we have freedom in Christ to make responsible decisions in accordance with God's word and a biblical moral value system. Obviously, even when something is created for good, it is not always good or beneficial, especially when it has a grip on us. When your teens' sexual activities become inappropriate and harmful to themselves and others, they are certainly on the wrong path.

The way to empower your teens to regain and retain their virginity is to help them bring their sexual choices in line with God's word. When your teenagers begin to distinguish, as Paul did, between what they are free to do and what is good for them to do, they will have reached an important level of moral development.

8

Just for Dads:
What Every Father Should Know

Where did your father spend most of his time when you were a child? Chances are he was at work, at least during those hours when you did most of your living and learning. The increasing absence of fathers dates back to the Industrial Revolution, the event that removed fathers from the home. We now have a generation of men who haven't bonded with their fathers and therefore know very little about bonding with their own children. Lacking a role model, they have little idea how to make an adequate emotional connection with their children.

There is much evidence that a warm, nurturing father positively contributes to secure healthy sexual identities among both boys and girls. Inversely, men and women who struggle most with their sexual identities report poor relationships with their fathers. While men who have poor sexual identities most commonly describe their fathers as cold and distant, women with similar problems tend to describe their fathers as sexually seductive. Obviously strong fathering plays a key role in the healthy sexual development of both sons and daughters.

Role Commitments Which Hinder Strong Fathering

The modern father takes his role of economic provider seriously, committing himself to a lifetime of hard work. Since work is a male's primary source of status and identity in most societies, his emotional absence from the home continues to be a vicious cycle that is hard to break. The present generation of fathers are making efforts to do better, but trying to meet the emotional needs of their children usually means breaking new ground.

Many factors outside his control make it difficult for a father to develop deep bonds with his children. Even if a man decides to make fathering his priority, he will have to buck an entire social system. Our society still assumes it's the father's responsibility to be the bread winner. And because job demands have increased greatly, even when a father is home, he has much less opportunity to bond with his children. He must crowd his interactions with his children into a few hours at the end of a work day, when his emotional resources are at his lowest, or into increasingly busy weekends. He may attempt to invent or improvise shorthand symbols of connecting with his children, such as purchasing gifts, taking them on brief excursions, playing quick games, making jokes, and telling bedtime stories. While these efforts are commendable, the father runs the risk of becoming little more than an entertainer.

For many hours a day in the workplace, a father must be rational and under emotional control. This gives him few opportunities to learn emotional expressiveness and vulnerability which are important aspects of nurturing children. And when companies require geographical moves, seventy-hour weekly work loads, and extended late-night or weekend responsibilities, a quality family life is nearly impossible.

Even our legal system fails to recognize the importance of the father-child relationship: fatherhood is not an acceptable reason for deferring from the military; divorce courts generally give custody of children to the mother, relegating the father to a position of periodic visitor; fathers are cited for failing to support their children financially, but little is done about the children's lack of emotional support.

The problem of absentee fathering is not solely the fault of fathers. In order to commit to strong fathering, men must have the conviction and courage to oppose the barriers that have been set up by our society. It's a risky fight, for it might cost them their jobs, promotions, or reputations. Father absence will continue to have a damaging effect on the sexual growth and development of both sons and daughters unless brave steps are taken to reverse this situation.

Fathers and Daughters: A Delicate Interaction

The way a father relates to his daughter sets the tone for the way she relates to all males. When she is respected, valued, and loved by her father, she is likely to develop a positive self-image that enables her to form healthy relationships with boys. Girls need their fathers to affirm their femininity more during their teen years than at any other time of their lives. Knowing the trust and emotional affirmation her father has given her, she will expect similar qualities in the men she chooses to date and eventually marry.

Expressing affection for his teenage daughter can be difficult for a father. Even though he was able to freely give physical and emotional affection to her when she was young, he may pull back when his little girl becomes a young woman. A scene from the TV series, "All in the Family," will illustrate this point. Archie Bunker has been told that his daughter Gloria is dangerously ill. He walks into the room and sees her lying in her bed, apparently asleep. With quivering voice and tears streaming down his face, he begins to tell her how much she means to him and how much he loves her. Just then, Gloria sits up and exclaims, "Oh Daddy! I've always wanted to hear you say you love me! Thanks, I love you too." Taken aback, Archie recovers and snorts out of the room in anger, caught red-handed at showing his vulnerable feelings of love for his grown daughter. His culture and value system taught him to stop expressing emotional affection for his daughter when she grew up.

The tragedy in this scenario is that it is precisely during those teenage years that daughters need most to be affirmed by their fathers. When a father pulls away emotionally, the girl may attempt to find affection from boys. This is what happened for Sandy.

Sandy's father was busy twenty-four hours a day in his

business. When he was around, he ignored her but found time to go fishing and hunting with his sons. Sandy felt like an outsider; she had no idea how to relate to her father. When he did interact, it was usually to scold her for playing loud music while he was trying to watch TV. She desperately longed for his attention.

In junior high school, Sandy began running around with a group of girlfriends. They had slumber parties and sometimes necking parties with boys. Sandy enjoyed the attention of these boys; they made her feel attractive. She soon became known as the "easy one." The physical touch and affection felt wonderful, but it scared her too. The boys were always pushing her to go farther than she wanted. But their desire felt good, and she usually gave in.

Now Dad *did* pay attention. He grumbled when she had boys over, he'd switch on the porch light when a boy walked her to the door, he made disapproving remarks about the way she dressed. Sandy felt guilty around him, and things went from bad to worse.

Just in the nick of time, one of her friends invited her to a church service. There people responded with kindness, acceptance, and love. They showed Sandy the love of Jesus, and she opened her heart to Christ. She stopped running around with her old friends and connected with the church crowd. An older couple who taught the Sunday school class she attended took her under their wing. They simply loved the high schoolers they taught, opened up their home for parties and good conversation, and gave wonderful warm hugs of affirmation.

Sandy talked about her confusion over sexual feelings

and desires in the small group she attended. In this group she felt understood and supported. She was able to talk about her disappointing relationship with her father. Sandy became more comfortable with herself as a developing young woman and began wanting friendship rather than sex from the boys she dated. Her father became less reactive, and their relationship improved as well.

Father as Protector

A father is inclined to be more protective of his daughter than his son. While he may disapprove when his son is sexually involved with a girl, he tends to see it as his son's indiscretion. With a daughter, a father is likely to blame her boyfriend for their sexual involvement, since social norms still see the male as the sexual aggressor and the female as the one setting limits. It's easy for a father to imagine a scenario where a boy relentlessly badgers "his little girl" to go further and further sexually. Perhaps he remembers that he behaved in somewhat less than noble ways towards the girls he dated.

On the other hand, a father who believes all girls are seductive temptresses will tend to blame his daughter for her sexual involvement. He conjures up images in which she leads the boy astray, when in fact it may not be the case at all. The father becomes emotionally abusive, telling his daughter she is a slut, accusing her of enticing her boyfriend, and punishing her for things she didn't do or even think about doing. These reactions by a father can be most difficult to sort out. He assumes something about her that's really in him, giving the daughter messages that there is something dirty, evil, or bad about her. In reality, it's the father who has the wrong thoughts, but he projects them on to his daughter when she simply exhibits normal sexual feelings. These false accusations are damaging, and she is confused by her father's explosive reactions to her sexuality.

A father needs to work out his own reactions to his feelings about his daughter's growing sexuality, and she needs to know how much he loves her and wants to protect her from harmful sexual encounters. She needs to talk with him about the boys she dates, because she can learn much from him.

She's Developing Curves

Sometimes a father is aware of sexual attraction toward his daughter as she matures into womanhood. Her budding sexuality may make him a bit uncomfortable when she's running around the house in a night gown. He may be tempted to look a little too long out the window when she's sun-bathing. His first response, naturally, is to deny these feelings, but this is the worst thing he can do. Denial doesn't work, because these feelings will make themselves known in one way or another. An example comes from the classic film, "Rebel Without a Cause."

When a beautiful 16-year-old daughter kisses her father goodbye, he unexpectedly slaps her face. "You're too old for that!" he reproaches her. His extreme reaction obviously reflects his inability to handle his feelings of sexual attraction for her.

While most fathers will not be as harsh as this, unresolved sexual attractions for a daughter may even fuel flames of jealousy toward the boys she dates. A father may direct these fits of rage at his daughter, at her boyfriend, or even at his wife. Focusing blame on someone else protects him from facing his own issues with his daughter's sexuality. In raging at others, a father may be deflecting the rage he feels at himself about being sexually attracted to his daughter.

It's natural for a father to find his teenage daughter sexually attractive. Daughters are likely to have many of their mother's qualities, the very ones which attracted him to his wife. The healthy response is to recognize and accept these feelings, not to deny them. Discussing them openly with a trusted person (his wife, a friend, or in a small group) will help a father gain a clearer perspective on his feelings and find ways to be accountable for his actions.

A father needs to let his daughter know she is attractive. He can do this in the presence of his wife, by making a comment about how nice she looks or by giving her a warm, non-sexual hug. I remember being at our neighbor's house when their 18-year-old daughter Georgia walked down the stairs all dressed up for the senior prom. Ralph looked at his daughter with wide-eyed admiration and shouted, "Georgia, you look beautiful!" A young woman needs to feel she is attractive. An attentive, sensitive father gives his daughter a great emotional gift when he compliments and appreciates her appearance.

Stepping over a Sacred Boundary

When a father oversteps the sexual boundary with his daughter, he seriously wounds both her heart and her soul.

It's an extremely complex spiritual matter, because God never intended that a daughter be damaged in this way. Sexual assault of a daughter by a father is a tragedy that has grave consequences for the daughter throughout her life.

I can't tell you the number of women who have told heart-rending stories of not just fathers, but brothers, stepfathers, mothers' boyfriends, uncles, friends, or neighbors who crossed the boundary. For some, it was an inappropriate suggestive remark or look, a derogatory label, a coercive move, or a physical touch. Sometimes it appeared to be an innocent mistake, like a touch on the leg in the front seat of a car, or a hand dangled around the shoulder that lightly touched the breast. Sometimes it was a confusing tickle or an overstimulating wrestling game. But in *every* case, it was baffling and uncomfortable for the girl.

Here are some examples of sexual abuse from fathers that women have experienced: (1) "My father would come to the bathroom when I showered and would stare at me with a funny expression on his face." (2) "My father masturbated in front of me. He never touched me, but it scared me so much that I started locking myself in the bathroom every morning to get dressed for school. I was so afraid he'd approach me." (3) "I broke my leg and was home for two weeks. My father would come in to see how I was doing. One day he suggested rubbing my back, but then he started rubbing me other places. I screamed at him to get out of my room, and he did. But nothing was ever the same between us after that."

A father is in a position of power over his child, which makes it difficult for her to question his behavior.

When a father abuses this power, the wounds he causes can take years to heal.

The Father as Empowerer

Affirmation is one way a father can help his daughter gain a strong sense of independence and self-confidence. In a study of successful women in male-dominated professions, it was found that the one thing successful women had in common was a highly affirming and supportive father.

A strong father-daughter relationship makes it easier for a daughter to differentiate and separate from her mother. In this important stage of maturity, a girl begins to establish a separate sense of self. A daughter is best able to find her identity when she is secure in her relationships with both father and mother. A teenage girl with a poorly developed sense of self and weak personal boundaries is susceptible to unhealthy attachments with boys. She is less able to discern between emotional and sexual needs, less able to assert herself when sexual advances are made, and more inclined to lose her identity in her relationships.

It's vitally important that a father validate his daughter's feminine qualities and individual strengths, affirming her as capable, pleasant, assertive, pretty, athletic, smart, creative, warm, strong, gentle, caring, and so on. She needs to carry in her head a picture of herself as an intelligent, attractive, feminine human being. When a father really loves his daughter and lets her know it in healthy ways, a daughter is sexually self-assured, best able to resist unwanted sexual advances from boys, and has the capacity to enter into a healthy sexual relationship at the appropriate time.

Fathers and Sons: Double Identity Confusion

Fathers frequently experience their midlife transition at the same time their children are in the midst of adolescence. Both fathers and sons are struggling with identity confusion and inferiority feelings at the same time, which can make for double trouble between them.

Establishing a separate identity is an important developmental passage which an adolescent expresses by exerting independence and pulling away from his parents. If a father can accept his son's behavior, both can grow. If he can't deal with it because of his own identity struggles, he'll take his son's behavior as personal rejection. Sometimes a father going through midlife crisis may put additional demands on his children in order to keep things from moving so fast. This creates havoc, especially for the teenage son who is eager to have more independence.

Fathers and adolescent sons are experiencing just the opposite physiological changes. At a time when the son is developing heightened sexual capacities, muscle strength and bodily growth, the father is losing his strength as his muscles are shrinking and sexual endurance diminishing. A personal story will illustrate this point.

I taught my son to play tennis with me shortly after we adopted him at age 10. By the time he reached 16, we were quite evenly matched, and I was so proud to have found a great tennis partner for the rest of my life. However, when Joel was 18 and I was in my mid-40s, my

worst nightmare came true: he began to beat me consist-
ently. There were times when my competitive spirit,
combined with the fact that my body could no longer live
up to former expectations, made it difficult for me to be a
gracious loser. I was faced with being overtaken by my son.
I needed to accept my physically deteriorating body and at
the same time affirm Joel as a young man coming into his
prime. I reminded myself that I had matured in many other
ways at this point in life. When I was humble enough to
accept my own physical deterioration at mid-life, I was
able to enjoy our tennis matches without grumbling. Now
it's wonderful to have a tennis partner who gives his dad a
good game. We enjoy friendly competition, and he even
gives me a pointer or two that he learned on the tennis
team in college.

When a father feels impotent and questions his
masculinity, he will come to view his maturing son as a
competitor. At worst, he may even lash out when his son's
emergent physical and sexual virility threatens him. As
fathers, we need to affirm our sons as sexual persons and
model appropriate sexual attitudes and behavior.

Fathers are unhealthy models to their sons when they
make sexist remarks about women. While watching a
football game, Frank and his son Jeff see a TV commercial
which features a shapely young woman in a revealing two-
piece bathing suit. Frank blurts out, "Wow, look at those
jugs! I'd sure like to see more of them!" Frank is reinforcing
the obvious message in the commercial—it's all right to
view a woman as a sexual object.

In a multitude of ways, we fathers give our sons both
positive and negative messages about sex. Most of us

probably say nothing when television presents women as sex objects. Try to help your son evaluate what he sees. Comment on negative sexual messages: "She sure has a beautiful body, but I resent the way the commercial makes a sexual object out of her. What do you think?" Such a response is honest; after all, it's normal to feel attracted to beautiful women. But the response also points out the sexually inappropriate ways in which women are dehumanized.

Weak Bonding

Teenage boys are preoccupied with gaining a masculine identity. When a boy is closely bonded to his father, it is quite natural for him to model the masculinity he sees in his father. As father and son interact on a day-to-day basis, the son learns how a male thinks, feels, behaves, loves, and works.

When the emotional attachment is weak, boys attempt to prove their masculinity by conforming to exaggerated notions of what manhood means. They find macho male models to emulate in Rambo, James Bond, and the Terminator, who teach them to be strong, tough, cold, emotionally detached, and devoid of nurturing tenderness. In relation to females, these traits translate into being sexually aggressive and using sexual conquests as a way to prove manhood.

Although patterns of weak fathering exist in all segments of society, their debilitating effects are especially noticeable in female-headed impoverished families. Often boys from these homes seek to find affirmation of their masculinity in a male gang. Gang members typically prove masculinity by being tough, daring, and sexually aggressive. The slightest show of tenderness or consideration for a girl can be interpreted as weakness by other gang members. To be cool and detached and void of "feminine" feelings is the symbol of real manhood.

The popular media also offer negative models of male sexuality, especial in teaching boys how to relate to females. The *cowboy* version glorifies the strong, silent type who has difficulty relating to females on the emotional level. The *playboy* version views females as sexual objects waiting to be swept off their feet by the male's irresistible sexual prowess. Neither of these is a healthy model of manhood.

"Mamas, Don't Let Your Babies Grow Up to Be Cowboys"

A few years ago, the lyrics of this popular country-and-western song warned mothers that if a son follows in his father's cowboy footsteps, he'll grow up not knowing how to relate emotionally to a woman. Historically we have admired the cowboy as a symbol of masculinity—the strong, rugged, silent hero. Perhaps the best portrayal of the cowboy role can be seen in any one of the typecast roles played by actor John Wayne. Around women in his films, Wayne appears to be uncomfortable and tongue-tied, especially if he really cares for the woman. He is more comfortable around his horse than around women. Any display of affection is likely to be disguised, rarely issued in a revelation of "I really love you." Such exuberant displays of affection would be out of character for the rugged frontiersman who supposedly won the West.

Given the glorification of the cowboy role in popular culture, a boy needs to see in his father an emotionally sensitive man who can express his feelings, as well as sexual desires, to the woman he loves.

Fathers, Don't Let Your Sons Grow Up to Be Playboys!

Another male role that sprang into popular culture in the 1960s is the playboy. Although the playboy might be considered a modern version of the cowboy, it differs in that it calls for the male to be non-feeling but verbal and self-assured. A movie example of the playboy is James Bond. Bond interacts with women with a cool air of detachment. Women fall passionately in love with Bond, but he remains aloof. It is interesting to note that in the one film where Bond does fall in love with the heroine, she dies—no doubt the tragic consequences of a man becoming emotionally attached to a woman.

As reflected in the philosophy of his "bible," *Playboy* magazine, a playboy is a skilled manipulator of women, knowing when to turn the lights down, what music to play on the stereo, which drinks to serve, and what topics of conversation to engage in. The playboy reduces sexuality to a package deal that he can handle without thinking because it demands no responsibility. A successful encounter with a woman is when the bed is shared but the playboy emerges free of any emotional attachment or commitment. When playtime is over, the plaything is discarded in a manner befitting our disposable, consumer-oriented society.

This is the picture of intimacy that our sons are exposed to daily. It's followed blindly by adolescents who make sexual advancements towards girls as a sign of their masculinity. It's reflected in the language used to describe "successful" sexual encounters with girls. The boy who fails to "score" is in danger of having his sexuality called into question. Without an alternative model of masculinity, many males reach adulthood culturally conditioned to treat females as objects rather than as people.

In the face of these powerful popular images of masculinity, boys desperately need a strong alternative image of male sexuality. Fathers can and should intentionally be that kind of model for their sons. The absent and distant father syndrome has to stop somewhere. If our sons are to escape the pervasive influence of cowboys, playboys, and machismo, they need fathers who can show them what real manhood is all about. This, more than anything else, is what a father can provide his sons.

9

Just for Moms:
What Every Mother Should Know

In an 1878 newspaper column young men were given this advise. "Every son, 'Behold thy mother.' Make love to her, and make her your first sweetheart. Be courteous, gallant, and her knight-errant, and your nearest friend and bosom confident. Nestle yourself right into her heart, and her into yours. Seek her company and advice, and imbibe her purifying influence. Learn how to court by courting her."

Between Mothers and Sons

What do you make of such advise? I'm sure it sounds rather strange to you but emotional attachments between mothers and sons were common in the late 18th century. In fact, the lyrics of a popular song during the turn of the century proclaimed, "I want a girl, just like the girl who married dear old Dad." What would your son make of this sentiment?

145

It seems quite harmless to suggest that a boy court his girlfriend with dignity, respect, and honor like he would treat his mother. But the counsel to love her as he loves his mother insinuates that sexual desire for a wife is abominable. It's not surprising that during this particular period of history, passion was relegated to escapades with the "bad girl," but considered improper toward the girl one loved. Traces of this distorted view of marital sex is still evident in some marriages today.

What a challenge it is for us mothers to give our sons healthy messages about sex and marriage. Whether we have to combat messages from the eighteenth or twenty-first century, we must do a better job of presenting sex in a way that enhances the marital relationship. You can have a significant role in your son's attitudes, thoughts, and feelings about sexuality.

"Hi Mom! I Love You!"

This familiar expression of affection brings a smile to a mom's face. Whether it's a professional football player waving to his mother on TV, a young soldier sending a message home from overseas, a hardened criminal with "Mother" tattooed on his arm, or a Valentine card made by your first-grader, a son's affection for his mother seems to be deeply implanted in his heart. The bonding that happens between mother and son at the beginning of his life seems to capture him forever.

Bonding and attachment between a mother and her children naturally occurs during the first few years of life. But there comes a time when your son makes a transition from mother as his primary object of affection to father, who is his primary source of male identity. He detaches from his mother so he can make an identity attachment to his father. A daughter, on the other hand, remains attached to her mother since she is also her source of female identity. She quickly settles into her female identity and it is solidified through an ongoing relationship.

I'm suggesting that it takes an extra effort for a son to pull away from his mother. You probably first notice this during pre-adolescence when your son begins to resist your nurturing advances. He knows he will be mercilessly ridiculed if he stays too attached to his mother for too long. The thing he dreads most is to be called a "Mama's boy." He soon learns that he can break away from her by reacting vehemently to any expression of physical affection, especially in public. "Yuk!," he says as he shuns your kisses, hugs, or any attempts to coddle him in ways that will be interpreted as sissy behavior. Pre-adolescent boys (between the ages of 7-12) put each other down for doing anything that has the slightest suggestion of femininity. It's as if your son has discovered that the way he proves he is sufficiently male is to have a knee jerk reaction to anything female.

This developmental transition may be humorous at times, but it can also be distressful for the mother. It helps to recognize the rhythmic ebb and flow of the behaviors. The first zit, the voice change, a request for more privacy, are all signs that your young boy is developing into a young man. These signals bring forth a knowing smile to a mother's face, but also puts a little pang in her heart. He wants to be close one moment, then asks for space in the

next breath. He oscillates between attachment and detachment until he finds the right balance. It takes a great
deal of sensitivity to read the signals and respond
appropriately.

Sometimes his desire for affection will come through
subtle, hard to read messages, but if you fail to pick up on
it he may feel rejected. At other times, he'll accuse you of
forcing yourself on him and let you know in no uncertain
terms that he feels invaded. Anticipating these ups and
downs can keep you balanced as he works through this rite
of passage into manhood.

You can do more than sit back and bide your time
during this awkward phase by using your creative mind!
Nurturing him with a great meal when he's famished,
making a special cake for a celebration, or attending his
sports or music events are wonderful ways to show your
affection and support. You may even be able to sneak in a
hug or verbal expression of affection in private. It's
important that he doesn't feel completely cut off from your
affection. The truth of the matter is, once he's secure in
his male identity, you'll be able to express your affection
more freely again.

Something Suddenly Changes

It may be that the part of this transition that's
especially hard is that during the process of becoming
aware of his sexuality and masculinity, he is also becoming
aware of you in a different way. He begins to notice you are
a sexual person and not just his mother. The sexual

awareness between you is a sometimes strange but important time of understanding female and male sexuality.

Fred Winslow gives an account of the day he realized something important had changed between he and his mother. One evening, when Fred was about nine years old, he wanted to share what had happened at school that day, and enthusiastically burst into his mother's dimly lit bedroom while she was getting undressed. In that fraction of a minute, he knew he had done something wrong. She bluntly commented that he shouldn't be in the room, and he blushed and retreated. He expressed these thoughts after leaving her room:

> I was stumped. For some reason, I could not run into her arms and be held. The joy I ran into the room with had been replaced by spooky unease. How much I had wanted to kiss her ears, smell her powderiness, feel her fleshy presence and be lost in the infinite softness of her, making her laugh with my attentions. But now there was some boundary not to be crossed. My visual knowledge of her and her awareness of that knowledge checked my desire. A unity had been destroyed. A formerly unqualified haven, she had suddenly developed limits the nature of which were still unclear but whose emergence into reality had been thunderous.

Something had been lost in the discovery. When a sexual dimension enters the picture, it creates a new kind of boundary between a mother and son. Your relationship will never be the same. Because he is male, and she is female, the dynamic between them may be confusing. A mother may be aware of sexual feelings she has toward her son during this stage, much like a father does toward his adolescent daughter. When she looks at his muscular body on the beach or feels the strength of his developing body when he gives her a hug, it may surprise her to have a sexual thought or sensation. Such an awareness of a son's sexual self and her response to this is normal and shouldn't be ignored or denied.

Discussing this awareness with her husband or a trusted friend will help her normalize the feelings so she can continue to be affirmative toward his male sexuality. If she pulls away emotionally because she's uncomfortable with her feelings, her son may wonder what's wrong with him. It's so important that she notices and accepts what's *right* about his developing body. A mother can express her positive responses to her sons physical body by complimenting him on how nice he looks all dressed up for his Saturday night date, for example. He needs personal validation of his newfound sexuality just as much as a daughter does.

Keeper of the Rules

Do you find yourself thinking it's your duty to keep your son in line when it comes to sexual matters, rather than to think of how you can acknowledge and accept his sexual self? If so, you're no different than most Moms. Somehow we fail to accentuate the positive, especially when it comes to sex, but we're good at pointing out the negative. Let me give a personal illustration to show how I resisted the tendency to give a lecture and turned it into an affirmation of my son.

I heard Joel making comments about the beautiful, scantily clad dancers on the TV during football half-time entertainment. Instead of succumbing to my impulse to reprimand him for focusing on a girl's body, I decided to affirm this as a normal response. I made a comment something like, "Yes, Joel, you're really into beautiful bodies now that you're a teenager. It means you're really aware of the sexual side of yourself." Instead of shaming him, I helped him feel comfortable about his interest in girls and their bodies. There would be other times to talk about moral values, but this was a time to affirm his sexuality.

One of the amazing things about my relationship with my son is the freedom we've had to talk together about sexual matters. When he was younger he sometimes disguised his questions by saying his friend was in a quandary. Rather than banter him into admitting he was asking questions for himself, I used this as a perfect opportunity to talk about sexual decision-making from a biblical point of view. One thing I learned, through trial and error, was to make very sure we had a dialogue instead of me delivering a sermon. I believe it was as important for me to hear what my son was feeling and thinking about sex as it was for me to give my viewpoints.

When Joel was fourteen he once made an off-hand comment to me about what "women want from men." As we talked further, I found he had gotten this idea from a friend's erotic magazine. Instead of raking him over the coals about the magazine, we talked about this distorted view of women. He was interested to hear my perspective about what a girl wants in a relationship with her

boyfriend. I was glad he was able to ask me about it rather
than rely on a pornographic magazine for wisdom about
women.

My friend Gloria describes the time she talked to her
16-year-old son, Kevin. He was being pursued by Janie, a
14-year-old girl. Kevin was elated that this sexy girl
wanted to go out with him. She was coming on pretty
strong and they'd been studying at the library every day
after school. He was flattered, but found her obvious sexual
approaches a bit overwhelming. He admitted he was
turned on sexually by her and that it felt good. It was the
first girl who took such an interest in him.

Kevin came to his mother asking a question about an
anonymous friend, "What can a girl do if her father is
sexually abusing her?" He was careful to keep names and
events confidential, but Gloria was quite certain he was
talking about Janie. They discussed the sober facts about
abuse and obtained the telephone number of a community
counseling center. As they continued to talk, Gloria
helped Kevin understand how a girl in this situation would
be especially hungry for affection. It was at this point that
Kevin admitted that he was talking about Janie. He also
admitted how tempting it was for him to respond to her
sexual advances.

Gloria praised Kevin for the wisdom he was using in
responding to her with understanding but not taking
advantage of this situation. They talked further about how
confused Janie was about sex and that it would take a
mature person to really care about her in a non-sexual way
during this difficult time in her life. This also led to a
consideration of other ways he could respond to the sexual

feelings he was experiencing as a growing young man. She advised that he keep an active physical life through his school sports, and commended him on his involvement in his youth group, the student government, and various school activities that helped give him a balanced life.

The topic of masturbation came up and Gloria suggested that this might be one way to keep himself pure. Instead of taking advantage of a vulnerable young girl, he could find physical release of his sexual tension through masturbation. Kevin understood this was a better alternative than acting out his sexual feelings with Janie. He told his mom he'd been having wet dreams and they talked about this being a natural way for his body to deal with his sexual energy. It was a special occasion for Gloria to normalize and affirm his sexual development as well as to help him think about various alternatives to acting out his sexual awareness in inappropriate ways.

This discussion led the way for further spontaneous chats about sexual matters because Gloria was available to listen and offer wise counsel. She was able to help him embrace his sexual self in positive and constructive ways, which kept him from getting entangled in regrettable situations. Gloria, a mother who was comfortable with herself as a sexual being, responded to her son in a competent, loving, assertive manner. These qualities gave her son a positive attitude about sex and the expression of it.

What's a Mother to Do?

Establish a relationship with your son as a whole

person with feelings, thoughts, sensations, and actions. Show him that you are comfortable with yourself as a sexual person as well as comfortable with him as a sexual person. Honor the boundaries that keep your emotional and physical expressions comfortable and appropriate. You can combat the idea that manhood means being a cold-hearted, emotionally detached person who is devoid of tenderness. Moms have a different message to offer by defining manhood as a warm-hearted, emotionally attached person who is full of tenderness for others. They can do an excellent job of raising a son with a healthy sexual identity.

Between Mothers and Daughters

Conceiving, birthing, nursing, and cuddling a child expands a mother's awareness of herself as a woman. Her heightened appreciation for womanhood connects her at a deep level with her daughter, who is similar to her from the inside out. Poet Adrian Rich observes, "Probably there is nothing in human nature more resonant with charges than the flow of energy between two biologically alike bodies, one of which has lain in amniotic bliss inside the other, one of which labored to give birth to the other. The materials are here for the deepest mutuality and most painful estrangement."

Our Bodies, Our Selves

There's an element of freedom in the mother-daughter relationship as feelings and emotions are exchanged through the mutual experiences that link them together. Their very bodies that define them as female connect them in a special way. Menstruation, the wonderful event that initiates your daughter into womanhood, is something every mother shares deeply with her daughter. As she buds forth into womanhood, you are acutely reminded of your own growing-up process. Watching your daughter go through the same bodily changes you went through brings an affinity between the two of you.

Media messages concerning the female body have a way of distorting a young girl's picture of herself as attractive or not attractive. Although our bodies come in all sizes and shapes, our culture emphasizes the perfect, glamorous, well-endowed, female body. Females tend to be critical of every part of their bodies whether it be legs, hands, face, feet, breasts, or hips. When a girl finds her body unacceptable or loathsome she denies something essential about herself. It's not surprising that many girls judge themselves deficient and go to great lengths to live up to the ideal portrayed in the popular magazines they read. Your daughter can easily become preoccupied with what's wrong with her body rather than what's right.

Feelings about one's body are further exacerbated by the inhibitions she may have about her sexual development. Jennifer remembers how embarrassed she was when she failed to develop breasts at the same time other girls did, whereas Cindy was embarrassed that she developed earlier than most. Many young girls have no awareness of their basic sexual anatomy nor can they name their private parts. If a girl can't name and accept the very organs that define her as female, how can she have positive feelings about her sexuality? Our sexual identity is intricately tied to how we accept our physical self. If a girl doesn't feel good about her body, she can't feel good about herself. If we can't accept our gendered and sexual selves, we'll lack a healthy self-concept.

A Vital Role

Mothers can play a vital role in helping their daughters accept their bodies and their sexual selves. By communicating openly about physiology (using correct terms like vulva, vagina, clitoris) we give our daughters permission to view their sexual parts as good and natural. When your curious child begins asking about her body, this is the time to name it and claim it for her. I watched my friend Karen do this in a wonderful way with her 2-year-old daughter. Sarah had been poking her finger at various parts and naming them after bath time. "Yes, this is your nose, this is your ear, this is your vagina," explained my friend. It was comfortable and connecting for both of them.

So often, girls are given restrictive messages about their sexual parts. Whether spoken or unspoken the "Don't touch yourselves below the neck," is the attitude that says it's only the head that is O.K. No wonder it's difficult for a girl to affirm and embrace her whole body. When a mother encourages her daughter to become acquainted with her body and her sexual sensations on her own, she'll have a sense of ownership for her body. If she finds herself in an uncomfortable sexual situation, she'll have the courage and self-assurance to say no.

What a Transformation It Is!

The first time a young girl looks in the mirror and sees herself as a sexual person, it's an awesome realization. Reflected back to her is the image of a young woman with curves, a span in the hips, roundness of breasts, and pubic hair that seems to have developed overnight. The vitality she feels inside is a wonderful sensation she wants to share with her mother.

Yet, the transformation that changes a little girl into a young woman may actually put distance between her and her mother. That solid bonding of mutuality in the beginning of life is now challenged in adolescence as a daughter feels a need to establish a separate identity from her mother. Now she must begin the separation, just as her brother did at an earlier age.

A daughter often establishes her independence by relying more on her peers for emotional support. She no longer needs her mother in the same way, and the mother may feel she's lost her special place in her daughter's life. It can be a lonely time for a mother who must watch from the sidelines rather than be the pivotal person in her daughter's life. When a girl pulls away to be with friends, her mother may feel shut out for the first time. Her daughter seeks increased privacy, looks to her peers as a more reliable resource for what's acceptable, and increasingly questions her mother's values. Maintaining close emotional ties will be difficult during this important developmental stage. Once independence has been established, however, the daughter can let down the barriers, opening up new opportunities for emotional sharing and interaction between her mother and herself. A wise mother weathers this storm with patience and continued expressions of unconditional love.

Keepers of Their Conscience

Mothers never seem to lose their fervor for cautioning their daughters about sex. It may put the "fear of God" in a girl and protect her from making mistakes, but it also inhibits her. Some mothers give confusing messages about sexual expression such as, "Keep a boy interested, but don't give him too much; be a little sexual, but don't get pregnant; kiss but don't pet." Your daughter ends up guessing how much is too much, wondering how to manage being sexual without going all the way, and trying to figure out how to give and hold back at the same time. Of course, remaining silent about sex not only inhibits her but keeps her daughter ignorant and open to intrusion as well.

"What do you wish your mother had told you about sex?" was the question asked of 30-year-old women in a study conducted by Linda Brock and Glen Jennings. These women recounted that even though their mothers were by far the parent most likely to provide information about sex, their communication about sexual matters was disappointingly negative. Three-fourths confessed their first intercourse experience was unpleasant, coercive, painful, or boring because they didn't know anything about sex. The women who found sexual intercourse to be a positive and pleasurable experience had open, enjoyable, and comfortable discussions about sex with their mothers beforehand. They made conscious and responsible choices about being sexual and they felt emotionally prepared for it.

However, most daughters told war stories about the sex talks with their mothers, remembering key words like NOTHING, NOT, NO, NONE, or NEVER. Memories of strong negative messages flooded them and they learned very quickly that they shouldn't be questioning, thinking about or having sex. One woman remembered running to tell her mother the first time she noticed pubic hair, but when she took one look at her mother's face she couldn't bring herself to reveal the location of the hair, so she told her about her exciting discovery of underarm hair.

The thing nearly all the women wished for was an *indepth* conversation about sex in a open and comfortable manner. They didn't just want to hear her ideas about sex being wrong, but they wanted to know that making babies feels good and that orgasm is pleasurable. They wanted to know about specific topics such as birth control and anatomy but most of them just wanted to have their mothers give a positive message about sex.

I think back to the time when my daughter and I started talking about sex. I tried to let her know she could ask any questions and I would answer anything she asked. I wanted it to be a natural discussion and not a secret. Yet, how clearly I remember that day we took our long walk to the neighborhood creek for my planned sex talk. It was not as easy as I thought it would be and we were both uncomfortable at first. But we had opened up the topic and it seemed to get better as we went along. We both became less inhibited after that day and sex became a more normal, routine topic when talking together.

Most of us regret being kept in the dark and ignorant about sexuality when we were young. We know how important it is to give our daughters something different. What we wanted from our mothers and what our daughters want from us is more than understanding the facts of sex; we want to know about the good physical and emotional feelings that can be part of sex.

What's a Mother to Do?

Our daughters want more from us than an explanation about how a penis enters a vagina. They want us to endorse sex as a pleasurable act of affection and emotional intimacy. They need to be relieved of the myth that sex is a shameful expression of lust and to be told *with conviction* that it's a purposeful demonstration of love. Our daughters need to know they not only have the right to decide when and who to have sex with, but that we believe they are worthy and capable of making these choices.

A teenager who had been involved in sexual encounters with several boys said, "It would have been nice to know I could say no. . .because I never ever learned it was O.K. to say no to males when they wanted something from me. I couldn't say no to my father or my brothers and I couldn't say no to my boyfriends. I needed to know I didn't have to have sex to win a boy's approval." When she finally understood she had the right to say no, she could begin to take personal responsibility for her actions that led to constructive choices.

The best way mothers can help their daughters develop sound sexual judgment is by building their self-esteem and affirming them in their gender and sexual identity. We can model a healthy view of sex through comfortable expressions of warm, physical hugs and touch. We can help our daughters feel comfortable with a range of sexual expression in the context of a loving and trusting relationship. And we can define and demonstrate our belief in Christian values where sexuality is an integrated part of the whole person.

Coparenting: The Best of All Worlds

The best environment for sexual growth and development for both boys and girls is one that provides close bonding with a father *and* a mother. The balance offered in joint-parenting gives teenagers a head start when it comes to clarifying their sexual and gender identities. A clear sense of self prepares them for emotional and physical intimacy with others.

Diane Ehrensaft's book *Parenting Together: Men and Women Sharing the Care of Their Children* (1990), reports that when compared to non-coparented children, co-parented children display greater moral development, have less animosity toward the other gender, and are better able to develop strong friendship bonds with children of the opposite gender. Boys showed greater empathy, affection, and nurturance characteristics, and girls had a clear self-identity and could assert personal boundaries.

We believe that when *both* parents are actively involved in the lives of their sons and daughters, they become a strong force in helping them establish their identity and the capacity for intimacy, the two most important developmental tasks in a teenagers life.

10

Empowering Teenagers Toward Sexual Responsibility

Eric Fromm has noted that the goal of socialization is to get children to want to do what they have to do to. The goal of parenting is to empower children to be sexually responsible adults. Parents must do more than shake their heads and wring their hands about sexual matters, they must guide their teenagers toward sexual responsible behavior that is biblically grounded. If parents falter in this task, teenagers will surely falter in their task.

In this final chapter, we present an empowering model of parenting that will help you reach this goal. But, first let's consider two parenting approaches that fall short.

Too Little, Too Late? or Too Much, Too Soon?

Parenting our adolescent children is especially problematic because it's the precise time in life when they question authority most intensely. Independence is the password into adulthood, and teenagers are continually asking themselves, "Do I embrace or reject my parents' attitudes, beliefs, and values?" In response to their struggle for autonomy, parents sometimes exacerbate the situation by taking one of two extreme parental postures, (1) being too *restrictive* (too much control) or (2) being too *permissive* (not enough guidance).

Highly restrictive parents hold the reins too tightly, creating rigid structures that allow for little movement toward independence. It's normal for teens to resist such confining control. John's home was extremely formal and rules ruled the entire household. Emotions were repressed and guarded, sex was never a topic of conversation, and he lived under a great deal of criticism. The way John eventually freed himself from the domination of his overly rigid parents was to leave home at the age of 16. Gaining autonomy seemed an impossible task in light of all the rules of correct behavior. His sister, Jennifer, rebelled inwardly by pulling away from her parents emotionally. Unfortunately, her inward rebellion led to an unhealthy relationship with her boyfriend which she kept a secret from her parents.

Highly permissive parents, on the other hand, don't take sufficient hold of the reins, which creates a chaotic environment. These parents let their children make decisions for themselves before they're ready. They fail to give enough guidance and ambiguity about expectations, which forces the teenager to behave in increasingly extreme ways in search for suitable boundaries. The permissive environment of Christy's parents illustrates this point.

Christy asks, "Dad, how late can I stay out tonight?" Her father replies, "Use your own judgment, just don't stay out *too* late." When Christy comes home at 2 A.M her father is furious, but he still tells her to think for herself! She continues to test out the limits until she finally figures out how late *is* too late. In the process, she has not only gotten attention through her misbehavior but has put herself in compromising situations.

Too many or too few rules impoverish our youth. They need a balanced parenting style that empowers them toward adulthood. The transition from dependence to independence requires a home environment that is *flexibly structured.* Parents need to provide enough structure and enough flexibility so they can successfully achieve the goal of becoming responsible adults.

A Model of Empowerment

We believe that parents can play a vital role in moving their teenagers towards responsible sexual maturity through an *empowering* posture. An empowering model of parenting attempts to transfer the source of control from parent to teenager. Empowered teenagers become sexually responsible, not to please their parents but because it reflects their internal standards and values.

We need to guide as well as support our teens as they gradually assume greater responsibility for their sexual decisions. An empowering parent provides a good balance of *affirmation* (support and encouragement) and *guidance* (direction and limits) that moves them toward self-control. The goal is to get teenagers to internalize values to such an extent that they take rightful ownership of their behavior. The ingredients of empowerment are communication and delegation.

Communication Lines Open

Parents are smart enough to know that it is not enough to simply tell teens what to do, they must teach the values and principles behind the rules. Effective communication is a two-way dialogue that creates understanding. Teenagers learn best through discussions that empower them to think through answers rather than merely accept rules. It's personally empowering when they integrate their faith beliefs with their behavior.

Dialogue isn't a ploy to persuade teenagers to take on a parent's point of view, but it is offering a safe and respectful environment where they can tell moms and dads what they think and feel. It has more to do with listening than with talking, as well as honoring the thoughts and feelings that are verbalized.

Dialogue also assumes that parents will be heard and understood. It means we must state our point of view and give reasons for what we believe. Hopefully, when we honor our teen's perceptions and values, they will honor ours as well. The following story illustrates how this can happen.

The Thompsons woke up one morning realizing that Rick's girlfriend, Joni, had spent the night in his bedroom. The parents asked them to dialogue about this situation. Rick explained that he slept on the floor in his sleeping bag while Joni slept in his bed. Both Rick and Joni's

Christian value system to be celibate was clear in their minds and they were 100% sure they would keep this boundary even when sleeping in the same bedroom. Their thoughts, ideas, feelings and opinions were listened to, valued, and respected.

However, the Thompsons also had a point of view to be expressed and understood. There was no need to shame the young couple nor to insinuate that they could not be trusted, but there was a difference of opinion. Rick and Joni listened while Karen and Rob shared about a similar commitment they made during their own courtship. They told about the times each of them had been tempted to break the commitment, but how their mutual agreement had been honored. They were honest about the vulnerable times because sex was a powerful drive. They also affirmed that they kept their commitment by being careful about when and where they spent time alone. Their joint decision had empowered them to follow through on their vow and had provided solid trust in their subsequent marriage.

Their experience taught them that sleeping in the same room could put them in a compromising situation. For that reason they asked Rick to sleep on the couch in the living room when Joni spent the night in his bedroom. The young couple valued and respected the wisdom of the parents' counsel and agreed to the request without being defensive. Through the dialogue, the four of them reached a new level of understanding and intimacy.

Keeping the lines of communication open is the key to empowerment. Teenagers will be more willing to talk about their sexual struggles when dialogue is the avenue of understanding. You'll benefit from listening to your teenager, who is an expert on teen culture. When they're free to inform you about the sexual values, practices, and attitudes of their peer group, it will help you understand and have compassion for what your teenager is up against. You'll be able to give the extra support to back them up when they make sexually responsible choices.

Too often parents communicate through condemnation. Adolescents are especially sensitive to criticism, for to condemn their action is to condemn *them*! Shaming messages alienate and isolate, and soon teenagers build thicker and higher walls until we no longer can reach them. A parent's only way through the barrier is through nonjudgmental and nonthreatening interaction.

What About Anger?

Anger is inevitable in parent-teen relationships. It's a common emotion that occurs when parents are in a position of power at the same time that teenagers are trying to find their own power. Disagreement and dispute is a natural part of trying to become independent from parents. In the process, an angry encounter between you and your teenager may, at times, get out of control. Counterhysterics on your part only adds kerosine to the already hot flames. When hassles become explosive, you must have the presence of mind to delay talking until your emotions have cooled down. When parents "lose their cool," it's quite scary for teenagers, who want to know their parents can handle situations that come up between them.

Teens are especially nervous about your reaction to

their expressions of anger towards them. A teenager may quite easily yell out in anger, "I hate you!" Countering with reactionary anger will swiftly escalate into an angry shouting match of mutual hostility. A wise parent could say something like, "I know you're really feeling angry at me right now and it's O.K. to let me know how strongly you feel. I'm pretty angry myself. Let's take some time to cool off, come back in an hour to talk more about this."

Feelings should not be forbidden or dampened, but dealt with constructively. Communicating about the angry feelings is the path toward reconciliation. Teenagers need a model that teaches them how to manage relational stress, not how to get caught up in the escalation. If you've gotten upset and lashed out at your teenager, a simple apology will go a long way to gain his or her respect. Saying something like, "I'm sorry I took my anger out on you. It was unfair and I regret what I said," gives them a chance to forgive you for your failures, just as they need you to forgive them for theirs.

Availability is the way to keep the communication lines open. Parents should make themselves available by picking up on clues, being interested in teenagers' lives, and listening carefully when they talk. It's amazing how often parents do not really listen attentively, and teens are very sensitive to parental *in*attentiveness. They pick up on the fact that you're pretending to be interested when you're not. Half-hearted listening is personally offensive and easily detected. You need to be critically aware of your listening habits, for if you're unknowingly communicating a *dis*interest in what they have to say, they'll soon stop talking, effectively cutting off all communication.

Delegating Personal Power

Delegating is the process that gives teenagers the ability to be responsible for their own behavior. As a teenager demonstrates increased maturity in making decisions, parents will give more latitude. When teenagers begin to internalize their values, they no longer require constant guidance. Self-affirmation is the internal reward that comes from living out a life that is consistent with their personal value system.

Parents can affirm their belief in their teenagers by giving them sufficient freedom to be responsible for their decisions. It's a matter of letting go and giving them your blessing. Even when you have some doubt about their complete readiness to take on a particular responsibility, you can empower them by letting them try rather than holding them back with your doubts. Lack of confidence in them is what keeps them dependent and doubting of themselves.

Delegating tasks and trusting teenagers to be responsible is a bit risky. Empowerment does not always go in a perfectly steady direction. Predictably, there will be times of regression and stagnation on the way to full maturity. They will undoubtedly make mistakes in the process of becoming completely trustworthy. Yet, there comes a time when you can no longer rescue them from their actions. The empowering principle says they must learn from their mistakes and deal with the consequences of their behavior. When parents have kept the communication lines open and teens have been equipped to ask critical questions of themselves, they are propelled in the direction of responsible choice.

This happened with Rick and Joni, who are now graduate students. They've remained committed to their vow of celibacy, but their parents are no longer monitoring this decision. Rick occasionally spends the night at Joni's apartment and they're following through on the practice of Rick sleeping on the couch instead of in Joni's bedroom. They've been empowered internally with the power of the Holy Spirit to live out a life that is consistent with their Christian belief system.

What About Conflicting Values?

Empowered teenagers will sometimes hold values that differ from their parents'. When this happens it's often hard to maintain an open attitude toward them. In fact, parents may be stricken with terror when their childrens' values push them in a more liberal direction than their own. Responding out of fear or worry will never get you anywhere, however, for offering advice when your own emotions are in high gear will be less than fruitful. You must compose yourselves and listen. Perhaps a simple comment that acknowledges how difficult it is to make moral choices in today's world will suffice for that moment. It also helps to remember that life is tumultuous for teens and they need to be able to express attitudes that seem perfectly sane to them even when they seem pretty far out to you. Often, they're spilling out what they are thinking at the moment and it's not necessarily what they're planning to do. In fact, they're often reflecting what they've heard from peers and it's still a working hypothesis rather than a foregone conclusion.

After you've had some time to listen, you can come back later on in the day and broach the topic again. Such as, "I've been thinking about what you said and I'd like to bounce some ideas off you about it. Are you game?" This isn't meant to be a debate, but rather to ask some provocative questions that will encourage deeper thinking. While you cannot force a value system into their minds, you can help shape and develop how they're thinking it through.

If kids think parents are trying to control their thoughts, the only thing they can do is to reject their authority. Empowering them to make their own choices and live with the consequences eases the strain of the power dynamics between parents and teenagers. Parents can also keep their teenagers accountable to themselves by making certain they face the consequences of their choices, rather than rescuing them.

Empowered teenagers are able to make responsible decisions because it's in line with what *they* want for themselves rather than because they're trying to please their parents. When they are empowered, your job is done, you can breath a sigh of relief and give yourself a pat on the back for a job well done. Ideally, by the time your teenagers leave home you'll be relating to them as adult friends rather than as parent and child. Just as Mark Twain was surprised at how much wiser his parents became between his 18th and 22nd birthday, you'll be surprised at how much your teens have grown as well.

The Best Kept Secret

Parents have the secret of what it takes to establish and maintain a quality sexual relationship. They must not buy into the widely held notion that adolescents in their sexual prime know more about sex than parents do. If parents give more sexual status and potential to their teens than they do to themselves, they're only perpetuating that myth. And believing this myth will leave parents insecure, hesitant, and ineffective to impart the deeper knowledge they need to tell their teens about sex.

Young people, in their eagerness to have sex, are ignorant of the deeper meaning of the relationship. When you think about it, teens have not matured to the place where they have enough of a self to give to a partner in a total self-giving way. Even though they may know the mechanics of sex, they're ignorant when it comes to the emotional intimacy between two people that leads to satisfying, passionate sex. Parents have that missing piece of the sexual puzzle. It's the best kept secret that needs to be told.

A teenager's tendency to focus on the genital aspect of sex leaves a major part of them untouched. The essential self remains hidden, sometimes never to be found. Only when the genital experience is part of the greater mutual discovery of a person, is it truly gratifying sex. It usually takes years in a committed relationship to discover this. Young people simply haven't lived long enough to know and love another person in a way that transcends a genital experience into an unparalleled union of exquisite communion.

Parents have much to offer their teens about the emotional rewards of intimate, passionate sex that develops through a long-term relationship. Once you recognize what you have to give, you'll be confident to tell what you know. If your teenagers will listen, they'll have reason to delay intercourse until they're mature enough to achieve this relational potential. Hopefully, they'll have more respect for their maturing process and give themselves more time to achieve that kind of intimacy with the person they choose to marry.

Putting It All Together

Unconditional loving leads to empowerment! It means giving grace to your teenagers when trust is broken and mistakes are made; it means reestablishing trust by forgiving and accepting each other; it means encouraging, equipping, guiding and then letting go and believing in them as they discover their own way; it means continually making yourselves available for intimacy as your teens grow into adulthood.

We look to God, the author and finisher of our faith, we look to Jesus who reconciles and restores, we look to the Holy Spirit who empowers and sustains, and we pray for ourselves and our teenagers that each of us becomes all we were created to be as sexual persons. We end this book with a prayer for you and your teenagers, adapted from "Thank God For Sex," by Harry Hollis, Jr.

Sex is your good gift, O God.
  To enrich life,
  To continue the race,

    To communicate,
    To show me who I am.

Sex is your good gift, O God.
    Help me keep it good in my life,
    Help me be open and honest about it,
    Help me protect its mystery,
    Help me keep it a meaningful part of my life.

Sex is your good gift, O God.
    Thank you for your unconditional love,
    Thank you for your mercy and forgiveness,
    Thank you for your empowering spirit,
    Thank you for your intimate love.

We Thank You, Oh God for the good gift of sex!